GIVE ME A BOOST!

THE UNDER-RESOURCED ENTREPRENEUR'S HANDBOOK FOR GROWING & SCALING YOUR BUSINESS

JACKIE P. TAYLOR

Give Me A Boost!
The Under-Resourced Entrepreneur's
Handbook for Growing and Scaling Your Business

HOV Publishing a division of HOV, LLC.
Bridgeport, CT 06605
Email: hopeofvision@gmail.com / www.hovpub.com

Cover Design: Success Ladder Enterprises LLC
Contact the Author: Jackie P. Taylor at info@jackiePtaylor.com

For further information regarding special discounts on bulk purchases, please contact: Jackie P. Taylor at info@jackiePtaylor.com

ISBN Paperback: 978-1-955107-81-5
ISBN Hardcase: 978-1-955107-50-1
ISBN ebook: 978-1-955107-49-5

Printed in the United States of America

This book is dedicated to my parents, Shoe-Booty and Cookie, as they were affectionately known in their youth. They provided the ultimate BOOST! by investing so much to ensure my sisters and I walked an easier path than they did.

I am forever grateful for the lessons, the love, the nurturing, and the sacrifices you both made. I endeavor to make you both proud every day.

TABLE OF CONTENTS

INTRODUCTION

A SMILE. A HEARTY LAUGH. Whether your right or left thumb is on top when you clasp your hands. These are all hereditary things – unique traits handed down from generation to generation.

I inherited my chubby cheeks and gift of gab from my father and my big calves (among other things) from my mother. These characteristics were inherited through genetics. But what about the things that are *not* inherited through genetics? Traits passed down through the generations as part of a family's survival.

Beyond genetics, cultures pass down various customs, beliefs, and practices contributing to families' survival.

- Some examples include:
- Traditional recipes and cooking techniques
- Religious rituals and ceremonies
- Cultural dances and music
- Stories and folklore
- Proverbs and sayings
- Embroidery and other crafts
- Farming and agricultural techniques
- Traditional medicine and healing practices
- Dress and fashion styles

These things may not be encoded in our DNA, but they are still deeply ingrained in our identities. They are often seen as vital to our cultural heritage. By passing them down to the next generation, we ensure that our culture and families can continue to thrive and evolve.

I have many memories of our dining room table in Brooklyn, NY. I grew up middle class in East Flatbush and recall our dining table being the center of the first floor in our semi-attached, single-family home. In our 'shot-gun style' layout, you'd walk in the front door to the porch, the living room, and the dining room, just before entering the kitchen. Here, we ate, did our homework, paid bills, and met with vendors trying to sell my parents something – it was our 'conference room.'

In the dining room, my parents reviewed our report cards. The brightest light in the house was the chandelier over the dining table. Whether it was good news or a woeful report, the dining room was where it was inspected with operating-room-level lighting by De-De (what we called my dad —pronounced Deh-Deh). It was also where my dad shared investment advice with us girls.

When we started a new job, it was at this table where De-De explained and reviewed our benefits elections and 401k or 403B enrollment forms. The dining room table was where De-De made me present my first business plan for JP Marketing Services, when I asked my parents for a startup 'loan' at 19 years old.

This was before 'financial literacy' was taught in schools or as part of robust summer enrichment programs. Though it felt like torture, I soon realized De-De's advice was valuable wisdom that not every kid was lucky enough to receive. You see, De-De had me later in life. He was born in 1927, and most people thought he was my grandpa when I joined him for bring your child to work day! He started his first business at eight years old as a shoe shine boy, delivering newspapers. He eventually earned his own paper route and hired his friends to work for him to cover more territory. He was motivated at this young age while growing up in the South by "needmo." I'd ask, "What is 'needmo'? He'd reply, "Well, I'd wake up and need mo' of this and need mo' of that! So that was enough to get me out and working!"

I appreciate that my dad maintained his humor even in the bleakest of times. Sometimes, it might be awkward to others. Still, it's the best coping mechanism I've seen yet. As I've matured, I realize I inherited that from him too.

De-De had to drop out of school in the 6th grade to support his very young mom, who had him after being raped at 14 years of age by the man in the household where she was a domestic worker. They had very little and often lacked the basics, like food and a warm place to sleep. My dad would talk about not having enough money to buy clothes and shoes, so he'd wear second-hand clothes. Once, he could only find one shoe and one boot that fit, so he wore them both. That's how he earned his nickname. Folks would yell, "Hey, here comes Shoe-Booty" when he'd deliver his newspapers.

Let's just say, De-De had been through some things! And his experiences shaped his perspective, tough exterior, stubbornness, and burning desire to raise his children to have so much more than he did. His wisdom was invaluable. I'll share some of his nuggets with you.

He'd talk to me about "The SBA" and how they helped fund his and my mom's soul food restaurants.

He taught me about motivation: "You can't stay up all night and sleep all day!" if I ever tried to sleep until after

9 am on a Saturday, after staying up late on a Friday night. Saturday mornings were for house chores!

He taught me work ethic: "As soon as you're able to get working papers, get a job so you can pay your dues" OR 'Go in before your boss and leave after your boss."

He shared the key to getting promoted, "Ask for extra projects so you can show your worth."

He taught me financial literacy: "It's not what you make... it's what you save".

He taught me the key to getting promoted while staying humble: "You have to kiss ass until you can kick ass!"

And if I ever felt down on myself for any glimmer of bias at work or imposter syndrome, he'd remind me: "You pull your pants up in the morning just like they do! There's nobody there better than you!"

I share this story of my father because it is an example of the impact that historical injustices in the US, systemic racism, and educational disparities have had on many people, including me. Though I am very grateful for what I have been able to inherit from both of my parents, I can't help but wonder what Shoe-Booty's potential could have been if he had not been born Black in America in 1927. If his mom had not been raped and forced out of her childhood into a mother role for which she was not yet ready.

Yet, despite all these challenges, De-De and Cookie raised three successful, happy college-educated children who wake up every day trying to help others. A Psychotherapist, a Clinical Nurse Specialist-RN, and a Partner in a global billion-dollar firm whose cup is filled when she mentors emerging founders!

It is a true blessing that my parents' ability to overcome educational disparities, racial and gender discrimination, and segregation has resulted in them developing an unparalleled resilience that they have passed down to their children. As a Black woman, I am incredibly proud to have risen to the level of Partner in a prestigious, multinational organization. Throughout my career, I have provided counsel and advice to numerous C-suite executives from some of the largest corporations in the world, as well as government leaders from some of our largest cities and states in the US.

While I used to take for granted my skills in strategic thinking, quick information synthesis, and oratory skills, I soon realized that not everyone possesses these talents. I've learned to lean into my gifts, which has resulted in significant dividends for me, my family, and the organizations I've worked for over the years. In addition to my desire to help people, I have also been able to leverage my skills and gifts to make a meaningful impact in the government sector and help many emerging business founders find their way. I often use the term 'emerging business' because the term 'small business' can be very limiting language and language is powerful. Seeing their growth and progress has been extremely rewarding and is a driving force for me writing this book.

While we should always commend and elevate success stories in spite of adversity, we must be careful not to normalize struggle. Constant struggle is exhausting. As someone who has struggled relentlessly, I have developed a sense of fatigue that is prevalent within many Black and Brown entrepreneurs. The culture of praising the struggle and the accompanying mindset is traumatic and stressful.

Entrepreneurs of color should not have to work twice as hard as their white counterparts, or literally risk death, to have access to the same opportunities. We must acknowledge the unique burden that Black and Brown entrepreneurs carry in order to appropriately address it. The need to BOOST! your energy is critical for any business founder looking to grow and scale, but it has a unique resonance with entrepreneurs of color, as explored in Chapter 4 of this book.

My story is your story. My gifts are your blessings. Give Me A Boost! and the Business Boost Society is my ministry, my impact, and - God-willing - my legacy for historically under-resourced entrepreneurs.

Your prosperity is my legacy. I pray that you leverage my inheritance to create generational wealth beyond today's imagination.

Our smiles, laughter, and how we clasp our hands are hereditary traits. However, other cultural practices that promote economic prosperity and generational wealth are passed down from generation to generation. For example, some families pass down their knowledge of entrepreneurship, teaching their children how to start and run a successful business. Others pass down training in a particular trade, giving their children the skills needed to work in a specific industry. Additionally, some cultures emphasize the importance of saving money and investing wisely, passing down methods for building wealth over time. Still, others believe in the power of owning property and passing it down to future generations, thereby building generational wealth.

What things did you inherit? Both genetic and cultural?

____

____

____

____

____

____

What do you wish you knew more about? What nuggets of wisdom do you wish you had learned sooner?

____

____

____

____

____

____

____

____

The cultural practices promoting economic prosperity and generational wealth may vary between families and cultures. Still, they share the common goal of ensuring the success and security of future generations.

Unfortunately, many historically under-resourced entrepreneurs and communities have often been deprived of these cultural practices and opportunities to build generational wealth. This can be due to various reasons, including the slave trade, systemic racism, lack of access to education and resources, and limited exposure to successful role models within their community—to name a few.

Many Black, Latinx, and women entrepreneurs face significant challenges when accessing business capital and funding. According to a study by the National Bureau of Economic Research, Black-owned businesses are three times more likely to be denied loans than white-owned businesses, even with identical credit scores and financial profiles. This lack of access to capital can make it difficult for entrepreneurs to start and scale their businesses, hindering their ability to build generational wealth.

Additionally, historically under-resourced entrepreneurs may not have access to the same networks and resources as their mainstream counterparts. They may not have connections with successful mentors or access to entrepreneurship training programs that can help them develop the skills they need to succeed. This can limit their ability to grow their businesses and compete in their industries.

The adage, "It's not what you know, it's WHO you know," can be damning for founders of color who don't have the network their white male counterparts have.

The lack of access to resources, networks, and cultural practices that promote economic prosperity and generational wealth can put historically under-resourced entrepreneurs at a significant disadvantage. Addressing these systemic inequalities is crucial for promoting a more equitable entrepreneurial ecosystem.

Without the benefit of a 'rich uncle,' where do these enterprising founders turn for help, guidance, start-up funding, or the relationships necessary to start, grow and scale a business? They (and you) need a BOOST! And this book is the start.

For clarity, the term 'rich uncle' is an idiom used to describe a hypothetical wealthy relative, usually an uncle, willing to provide financial assistance or inheritance to the person. This phrase is often used lightheartedly to suggest that someone has financial security, business knowledge, or access to wealth due to their relationship with a wealthy family member – though not necessarily an uncle. I am grateful for the experience and insights I was able to garner from my father. He taught me so much despite not having a college education and obtaining his GED in 1945 while in the army. He went to the School of Hard Knocks! Most of us do not have someone with experience to hand down entrepreneurial insights. If you had someone in your life to fill this role, what was that person like?

If you did not have someone to fill this role, describe what a 'rich uncle' would have looked like for you. What experience would they have? What background? What financial situation would they be in?

WHO needs a BOOST?

Being a Black, Latinx, Native American, or veteran business owner has most likely disadvantaged you from the start. Even women business owners are often up against some of these same barriers. For example, let's say you are a first-generation entrepreneur and didn't inherit your business from your parents. This means that you didn't grow up getting familiar with how to run a business. You had to learn that on your own. You didn't inherit a client list to give your company a solid start. You had to develop your own creative marketing plan to gain customers. You probably didn't receive startup money from a rich uncle, so you scrambled to find funding elsewhere. According to data, individuals who are non-white possess a reduced amount of total assets, resulting in fewer savings and resources to utilize as loan collateral. Additionally, obtaining loans is more challenging for women, especially women of color, compared to men.

Traditional attitudes have put women at a disadvantage when it comes to seeking investors. In 2018, only 2.2% of venture capital was received by startups founded by women, a statistic that worsened to just 2% in 2021. Nonetheless, the emergence of more female investors in 2021 has caused a positive trend, as they have shown a strong inclination towards investing in female-led businesses.Many hope this trend will continue. However, as of late, PE and investor activity have significantly slowed. Interest rates are elevated, and the capital markets have tightened for EVERYONE-including those interested in investing in historically under-resourced businesses. This means Black, Latinx,

Native American, Veteran and Women owned businesses risk being disproportionately impacted.

Another obstacle you may have faced is that the community where your business is located may not be considered affluent even though it does not reflect the spending habits of its residents. A 2019 Nielson report indicated that Black consumers in the US have a buying power of $1.3 trillion, and Hispanic consumers have a buying power of $1.5 trillion. The perception of some lenders is that many of your potential customers may be unable to afford your higher-end products or services based on demographic information by zip code. Banks consider these negative factors when you try to get a loan.

Despite the challenges, your burning desire to make your business successful is probably the reason you chose this book. Suppose you are a minority business owner—Black, Hispanic, Latinx, Native American—or a veteran or a woman. In that case, you are already up against tough challenges on top of the typical ones that every emerging business owner faces. This makes growing your business a lot harder. Yet you can overcome every obstacle with the right tools.

YOU MADE IT THIS FAR! You started from scratch with limited advantages except for your abilities and sheer determination. You got your business up and running! More important, your business has remained viable, perhaps even growing. Even if your revenue has been flat, you are still in the game! **This shows me that you have what it takes to grow and scale your business exponentially. You can scale it even further with the right knowledge, resources, and support.**

All the founders I speak to want many of the same things. They want to create and build something bigger than themselves. They want to birth an idea that will benefit the world. They want to make money and improve their quality of life and that of their families. They want to create generational wealth.

~They want to leave a LEGACY~

Let's look at five reasons leaving a legacy may motivate entrepreneurs. Write down what each of these reasons means to you. Does it resonate? Take the time and be honest with yourself. You don't need to share this with anyone else. Note something specific in each of these categories for your own entrepreneurial journey. Add your own. Understanding your WHY before embarking on a journey of growing and scaling your business is essential.

1. **Immortality:** Leaving a legacy is a way for people to be remembered after death. It gives them a sense of immortality and ensures that future generations remember their names and achievements. What do you want to be said about you and your journey? How do you want to be remembered?

____

____

____

____

____

____

2. **Impact:** Many people want to impact the world positively, and leaving a legacy is one way to do so. By contributing something meaningful, such as a charitable

foundation or invention, they can make a lasting impact on society. How will you leave the world better than you found it?

____

____

____

____

____

____

3. **Family:** For some, leaving a legacy is a way to provide for their family and ensure they are cared for long after they are gone. This may involve leaving behind financial assets or a strong reputation that benefits future generations. Is building generational wealth important to you? Explain.

____

____

____

____

____

____

4. **Recognition:** Some people strive for recognition and praise from others; leaving a legacy is a way to achieve this. By creating something noteworthy, they can gain the respect and admiration of others. From whom would you appreciate recognition?

____

____

____

____

5. **Personal fulfillment:** Leaving a legacy can provide personal fulfillment and satisfaction. It allows people to reflect on their accomplishments and feel a sense of pride in what they have achieved. How will growing this business make you feel more fulfilled?

Now that you have defined your WHY, you're ready to get down to brass tacks! Here is an early overview of the upcoming chapters and topics covered.

Chapter 1

BOOST! Your Business Readiness

Stay ready, so you don't have to get ready! This chapter discusses the importance of risk management for businesses looking to grow and scale. Risk management is not just an exercise for global, well-known brands — it's an essential business element that should start from day one. Strategies to reduce risk and uncertainty are outlined in a way that is easy to understand, including forming contingency plans, diversifying revenue sources by leveraging the Four C's, and establishing and tracking key performance indicators (KPIs). Businesses need to have these preparations in place to ensure successful growth.

Chapter 2

BOOST! Your Marketing and Branding

This chapter explores how historically under-resourced businesses can effectively market and brand their products or services. It explains the importance of devising a marketing strategy, creating a solid brand identity, and leveraging social media and other digital channels to maximize visibility. It outlines practical strategies, such as taking advantage of low-cost online tools, analyzing consumer trends, and utilizing influencers, to ensure that an under-resourced business can successfully promote its products and services.

Chapter 3

BOOST! Your People Resources

To ensure the success of a business, it is necessary to form a solid and competent team. This chapter discusses methods to recruit, keep, and train talented employees. It is impossible to carry out all tasks alone. To succeed, businesses should ensure their teams comprise trustworthy, competent people.

Chapter 4

BOOST! Your Energy

Protecting your energy as a founder must be a priority. After all, health is wealth! This chapter emphasizes the importance of business owners managing and boosting their energy levels to ensure they stay motivated, productive, and successful in their business endeavors.

Chapter 5

BOOST! Innovation and technology

This chapter clarifies that innovation and technology are crucial to success and growth. It looks at three main ways to create new business models, use emerging technologies, and develop new products or services. Each aspect offers different degrees of potential, so staying up-to-date and knowledgeable about the constantly changing digital world is essential. To help with this, the chapter emphasizes the value of utilizing online resources for research and development.

Chapter 6

BOOST! Partnerships & Collaborations

This chapter will explore how your emerging business can form strategic partnerships and collaborations to foster growth and scalability. This may involve working with suppliers, customers, or other businesses in the industry. 'Boost! Partnerships & Collaborations' is about embracing a spirit of abundance. There is enough business available for you and your strategic partners to be wildly successful.

Chapter 7

BOOST! Your Access to Capital

Under-resourced businesses face many unique challenges—one is access to capital. This chapter delves into the difficulties historically disadvantaged businesses may have when seeking the funds they need for progress and expansion. It examines various methods for obtaining capital, including crowdfunding, grants, loans, and equity investments.

Chapter 8

BOOST! Your Grittiness

This chapter will explore the power of grit and determination in entrepreneurship. We will deep-dive into the characteristics that make some entrepreneurs successful and why developing those qualities within ourselves is crucial. It takes more than just a good idea or a desire for success to make it in the business world. We will examine the stories of successful entrepreneurs who have faced seemingly insurmountable challenges yet persevered through grit, and a refusal to give up. We will explore the mindset and habits that allow entrepreneurs to thrive in the face of adversity and how we can adopt these traits to overcome our challenges. Ultimately, we will learn that success in entrepreneurship is not just about talent or luck but about having the courage to get gritty and persevere through the most challenging times.

Chapter 9

BOOST! It's A Verb...So Take Action

This final chapter emphasizes the importance of taking action, even in the face of uncertainty, to move towards achieving your business goals. A checklist and thought-provoking prompts are provided to prepare your mind for action-oriented, forward movement.

This is your chance to achieve your dreams! If you integrate the wisdom from this book into your approach to your business, you will go farther than you ever imagined. So, what's stopping you? Start right now!

NOTES

-CHAPTER 1-

BOOST! YOUR BUSINESS READINESS

MANY FOUNDERS WILL HAVE AN idea and just start selling. They will spend more time being the product or service provider than planning for their business, forecasting revenue streams and targets, and developing a growth strategy. Ask many business owners how big they could grow; most will undoubtedly give vague answers. "Big," "Multi-million-dollar level," and "Worldwide!" are the most common answers, instead of a more precise "I'm working to triple my growth to $3 million in revenue in the next 24 months."

Can you appreciate the difference?

Though under-resourced entrepreneurs are severely under-monetized, most struggle to quantify their needs to grow their businesses and reach their targets. Many simply say they need 'money' or a 'loan' or 'customers' rather than "I'll need $750k for XYZ to meet our $3 million target in 24 months, which, based on my revenue projections for product X, we can repay in "Y" years."

When an otherwise competent, high-performing founder cannot clearly articulate their business's growth strategy, they risk appearing 'not ready' for the next level or credible investment. A solid business strategy and business planning can address this gap.

In early 2023, I will launch a campaign called 'Give Me A Boost.' I'm on a mission to talk to 10k business owners and ask them to clearly articulate what they need to BOOST! their business. Stay tuned on Instagram, Tik Tok, and Facebook for the responses. In the meantime, in the words of Will Smith: "Stay ready so you don't have to get ready!"

Are you indeed an entrepreneur, or are you self-employed? Is this enterprise one of several that you are starting simultaneously, or are you deliberate about genuinely focusing on and growing one business at a time before dividing your attention?

Being an entrepreneur and being self-employed is different

The main difference between being an entrepreneur and self-employed is that an entrepreneur starts and grows a business with a vision of creating something bigger than themselves, while someone self-employed is working for themselves without necessarily having a larger picture or aspiration for growth.

Entrepreneurs typically focus on scaling their businesses, creating customer value, and solving problems innovatively. They are risk-takers who invest time, money, and energy into their business to build something that can eventually run without their direct involvement in day-to-day operations.

On the other hand, self-employed people may work as freelancers or consultants and provide services to clients without necessarily trying to grow their businesses. They tend to work solo and rely on their skills and expertise to make a living without looking to expand or scale their business beyond a certain point.

While entrepreneurship and self-employment involve working for oneself, the distinction lies in the entrepreneur's focus on creating and growing a scalable venture and the self-employed's focus on providing services for personal income.

To become an entrepreneur, you must adopt an entrepreneurial mindset. You need to find ways to scale your business. You must think bigger and expect to take on much higher risk. In other words, you need to plan to grow your business *exponentially*.

Freelancers, plumbers, and aestheticians, for example, are usually self-employed. The owner is responsible for every aspect of the business, limiting how large the company can grow since there are only 24 hours a day and only so much one person can do on their own. An aesthetician may have a salon where she (or he) works alongside a few contracting beauticians. They can be successful, but this business model limits their growth potential.

On the other hand, an aesthetician who is an *entrepreneur* will rent out *all* the chairs to contracting beauticians. They may not be in the salon every day, since their goal is to grow and scale their business. They will be busy acquiring the next business or establishing a new revenue stream. Now that their salon is profitable, they can duplicate this successful model to create multiple businesses and/or multiple streams of income.

So, the question is: do you consider yourself an entrepreneur? If so, then you are *more* than just a business owner. You are a *visionary*, a *dreamer* who believes in your idea and envisions where your company can go and what it can become! You can see it expanding to have more influence, customers, and profits. You see how your one company can spawn offshoots that become successful entrepreneurial companies themselves. You know you and your team will benefit financially and personally if you can successfully multiply your business. You can hardly wait to instill your expanding vision into your people and light a fire under your company.

This is why this book is so valuable! The 'tried and true' guidelines in each chapter come from the personal experiences of wildly successful entrepreneurs. Their advice will save you from years of struggling because you didn't happen to know one crucial bit of information. It will prevent you from wasting money on business expansion ideas that don't work.

According to the Small Business Administration (SBA), around 80% of small businesses are solo or have no employees other than the business owner. Perhaps you are daring to transition from being a sole proprietor to an entrepreneur. You would think that at this early stage, you should brainstorm all the possibilities open to you. But no. The key to becoming an entrepreneur with multiple successful businesses is to **get super-focused on the one company you already have**. Successful entrepreneurs will tell you that this is the only way to determine if it is 'growth ready.' This means you must critique each part of your business and honestly decide whether it is boosting your business forward or keeping you stuck in a rut.

A handy business tool called **SWOT** (an acronym for **Strengths, Weaknesses, Opportunities, and Threats)** lets you pinpoint your business's strengths and weaknesses. It also informs you of available opportunities and reveals any threats that could tank your business. **This is vital information you need to know *before* you try to grow your business and become an entrepreneur.** By focusing on these factors, you can assess how successful your business is *right now* and what needs to change so that it can grow. Eventually, as an entrepreneur, you will use this business as a template for setting up future successful businesses. You must zero in on any issues and fix them before using this business as a model for future ones.

Too many business owners try to set up their Business Plan for Growth before they do a SWOT Analysis. This puts the cart before the horse because you will not have helpful information to build your growth plan unless you know what you're doing right or wrong. Suppose you are bleeding profits with your current business. In that case, you certainly do not want to duplicate that model when you try to expand. You will just bleed MORE profits. Instead, correct the problem that is causing the bleeding first. This is why it is critical that you do the SWOT first.

What exactly is a SWOT analysis, and why is it important?

A SWOT analysis is a tool used in business and marketing to identify and analyze a company's internal and external factors influencing performance. This analysis evaluates a company's competitive position in the market, helping to identify potential risks or rewards arising from any current or future business decisions.

Strengths are any company's internal characteristics that can give it a competitive advantage. These could include resources, brand recognition, customer loyalty, processes, etc. **Weaknesses** are any interior characteristics that could prevent a company from reaching its goals. These could include a lack of resources, outdated technology, lack of brand recognition, etc.

Opportunities are the external environment factors that the company could benefit from. These could be new customer bases, product expansion, technological advancements, etc. Finally, **threats** are also external environmental factors yet, in this case, those that could harm the company. These could include new competition in the market, changing customer preferences, new government regulations, etc.

A SWOT analysis is vital for any business because it helps them to identify the areas that need improvement and take the necessary steps to make the required changes. By understanding the areas of strength and weakness, your company can be better prepared to take advantage of any opportunities and to prepare for any threats that may arise in the future. Furthermore, it allows you to identify any areas of improvement which can help you stay ahead of the competition.

Overall, a SWOT analysis is an excellent tool for any business to improve its performance, stay ahead of the competition, and prepare for future market changes. This tool will help the company make informed and efficient business decisions to maximize its potential.

Gather all the available data related to your emerging business, such as financials, customer feedback, competition, etc. Make lists of your business's strengths, weaknesses, opportunities, and threats. Analyze the collected information and create a SWOT analysis. Develop strategies to address the identified strengths, weaknesses, opportunities, and threats.

The diagram below is a **SWOT Analysis Matrix**. Make a copy and start filling it in to get a clear and well-rounded analysis of your business. For more details and a downloadable worksheet, go to www.JackiePTaylor.com

Figure 1. A SWOT Analysis Matrix

Strengths	**Weaknesses**
What are your areas of expertise? What distinguishes your capabilities from others? What qualities do people identify as your assets?	In what areas could you enhance your performance? What areas do you lack sufficient resources compared to others? What are some aspects that others may view as drawbacks or deficiencies?
Opportunities	**Threats**
What opportunities are available to you? What market trends can you make the most of? In what ways can you convert your strengths into opportunities?	What are the potential threats that could affect you negatively? What are the actions being taken by your competitors? How can your threats lead to potential risk for you?

Strengths: Your business has many strengths because if it didn't, you would likely not be considering growth and expansion. Even if there are areas that can be improved, there are probably also areas of your business that make you unique, and memorable. These are your strengths and, in some instances, your differentiators. Think about what works well in your company: do you have great employees, or a product or service that sells well? Do you have fantastic customer service reps? Is your marketing bringing in new and repeat customers? Are you proud of your sales team? Also, think about the software programs you are using. Are they saving you time and frustration? List your company's strengths on the form.

Weaknesses: Be honest with yourself about your company's liabilities. For example, have you noticed that certain employees resist change and insist on doing things the old way (or their way)? Have you been ignoring possible profit leaks from sloppy record keeping, missing inventory, poor marketing ROI, and wasted time with inefficient logistics? Isolate the issues hampering your business and deal with them before moving toward growth or full fledged entrepreneurship. You may be surprised – a fixed weakness may become a strength!

Opportunities (external): Collect fresh demographic data about your customer base. The demographics may have changed in the past few years. You need to know the current income levels, gender, ages, education, housing and family makeup, etc., of your target market. While you are at it, gather psychographic data, too. **Psychographic data** is a type of data that describes the psychological characteristics, values, attitudes, interests, or lifestyle of individuals or groups. It is used in market research and advertising to understand consumer behavior or target specific audiences based on their personalities, interests, and motivations. Psychographic data can be collected through surveys, interviews, focus groups, or online tracking of social media or website activity. It provides insights into customers' buying habits, decision-making processes, and preferences, as well as their emotional and lifestyle factors that influence those choices. See what your customers are interested in, what they have been buying and why, and where they share their opinions about your products or services. Shifts in these groups of people may suggest new growth opportunities. In this section, jot down creative ways to reach new customers and keep existing ones.

Threats (external): One way to see what your competitors are up to is to browse their websites and read their customer reviews. This can give you an idea of their approach to the market and how their products/ services differ from yours. Go on social media platforms to read comments about their products and customer service. Also, take a broader view to consider the state of the economy and your vendors and supply chain.

Once you have fixed the internal issues holding your business back, assessed your potential customer base for the future, and decided what changes you need to make to prepare your company for growth, you are ready to grow your business!

Growing your emerging business into a larger one is a calling that can positively impact you, your family, and your community. With your commitment to growth, it can become much more successful than it is right now and be self-sustaining—something you can pass down to your children. If you want more, you must think like an entrepreneur. This means that your goal may include owning multiple businesses that are not necessarily all selling the same product but are built on the same successful business foundation. Let's talk about what it will take to build that successful foundation.

Being Ready to Grow and Scale

Growing a business means making it bigger, better, and more profitable by enticing new customers, introducing new products or services, or venturing into new markets. It's a gradual process that involves making small changes over time. **Scaling a business**, on the other hand, is all about rapidly increasing revenue and market share without incurring additional costs. This requires the use of technology, streamlining processes, pooling resources, and forming strategic alliances to achieve exponential growth. Growing and scaling a business are both crucial for its success. However, they require different methods and tactics to achieve.

To develop a business growth plan, it is essential to have a clear and concise mental picture of what exactly you are growing. Simply stating that you want to increase revenue or add employees is not enough. As the founder, you are the visionary and leader, and having a clear vision of your growth strategy is imperative. However, in order to implement your strategy, you must also have tactical clarity about what specific steps are necessary to achieve it. This will enable you to align your resources to the work at hand.

The Four C's

There is a technique called The Four C's that I use to help emerging business founders create a tactical basis for their growth vision. Keep in mind that after completing the Four C's exercise, you may feel excited but also overwhelmed. The goal is not to do everything right away or in a month, but rather to show you how big your enterprise could become in the next 1, 3, or 5+ years and motivate you to action. From there, you can deliberately lay the groundwork to achieve your vision, one brick at a time.

The Four C"s are

- Consumers
- Contracts with Government
- Corporate Clients and
- Collaborations

Let's discuss each of these categories. Document how you currently leverage this category. If you do not, how you could expand your customer mix either with your current product/service offerings or by creating new ones focused on this customer category's needs.

Consumers

One effective strategy is to target individual consumers in order to expand your consumer base. By reaching more people, you can increase your revenue streams and improve profitability. Satisfied individual customers can also lead to word-of-mouth recommendations to their friends and family, which can further increase your clientele. By building strong relationships with individual clients, you can create a loyal customer base that will provide consistent business over time.

____

____

____

____

____

____

Contracts with Government

Another option for expanding your customer base is to pursue government contracts, which offer lucrative opportunities for small businesses to thrive and grow. Although winning these contracts may take time, they can lead to major opportunities for long-term growth. Government contracts are available at the Federal and State & Local levels.

____

____

____

____

Corporate Clients

Targeting corporate clients can provide you with consistent revenue streams, as they often have access to more resources and high-value contracts. This can lead to long-term partnerships and sustained growth for your business. Overall, strategically expanding your customer base can be the key to your emerging business's growth and long-term sustainability. Businesses that work with corporate clients, as per a 2018 Forbes' report, experience more certain revenue streams as compared to those catering only to customers. The report highlighted that corporate clients offer a steadier income source for these businesses, given their higher spending power and tendency to indulge in longer contracts.

Collaborations

When a business works with other companies to collaborate or form a strategic alliance, it can benefit in many ways. Joint efforts can increase marketing efforts, helping to reach new customers and expand into fresh markets. Partnering with credible organizations can also help build brand recognition and enhance customer perception. Moreover, collaborating with a variety of partners can multiply the potential customer pool. By pooling resources, knowledge, and expertise, a business can offer customers more value. Partnerships show customers a company's commitment to customer satisfaction, building trust and loyalty. Accessing new markets through collaborations can lead to new streams of revenue and growth opportunities. This is so game changing for business growth, chapter 6 is fully dedicated to exploring this particular category.

____

____

____

____

____

____

Upon completion of the Four C's exercise, you may want to document a **Business Growth Plan** and consider it as your business growth **"template" that you can repurpose.** It will be a framework you can tweak to fit whatever new business enterprise you want to start next. You can use it to duplicate what works repeatedly and build your future- one successful start-up at a time!

The steps below are from Business.com. They will help prepare you to write your actual Growth Plan. In Step 3, allow yourself to dream bigger, beyond expanding your current business Leverage your work on the Four C's as an input into the growth opportunities. After you complete your growth plan for your existing business, implement it, and see your business grow, expect to reuse it—because it will be your template for starting more businesses!

My Growth Plan:

1. **Think ahead** – Evaluate your target market, your competition, and any previous company growth. Write down everything that has worked for you so far.
2. **Study the growth plans of successful businesses** – Do this before trying to write your own plan.
3. **Discover growth opportunities** – Research and brainstorm ways for your company to grow and for you to take the first step in your entrepreneurial journey. Suggestions are selling or creating new products, adding more services, exploring new markets, opening new locations, or even going global.
4. **Evaluate your team** – Assess your skills and those of your employees. This way, you can determine how much growth you can achieve using your present team and decide whether to hire people with specific skills or outsource during the transition. I provide a method for how to do this in chapter three- the 3 D's
5. **Find the capital** – Include details on how you will fund your expansion. Insights in this area can be found in chapter 7.
6. **Get the word out** – Review chapter 2 to detail how you intend to promote your business to increase its size and explain how your promotional strategies will change as your business expands.
7. **Ask for help** – Chapter 8 provides instructions on how to obtain guidance from accomplished entrepreneurs who have expanded their enterprises.
8. **Start writing** – Go to www.jackiePtaylor.com to get started.

I want to share Marcia Taylor's story with you:

Marcia, a single mother of three escaping an abusive relationship, went to work for a small Georgia trucking company with no training or experience in logistics. Here she worked hard and, over time, developed a relationship with her boss, JD Bennett. They would eventually marry. Both had a keen eye for investment, and in 1974, they decided to buy the company, which had 15 trucks and 30 trailers. They could purchase it on credit with only $500 to their name and become the new owners. Marcia prioritized creating a family atmosphere among their truckers, a decision that had a lasting impact. Unfortunately, JD suffered from severe emphysema and died shortly afterward, leaving Marcia as the trucking company's sole owner and CEO – at a time when women were not associated with the industry. To her surprise, her truckers pulled together and kept the company going through the tough times.

Marcia was determined to grow her business. She may not have known about the SWOT Analysis tool we use today that helps companies to find their Strengths, Weaknesses, Opportunities, and Threats. Still, she did recognize the stiff competition that her small company was up against. Perhaps it was because her background was not in trucking, or maybe it was her ability to think outside the box, but Marcia sought out unique opportunities that other trucking companies avoided. She had her trucks move agricultural equipment, rockets, ammunition, and explosives. Armed with these niche contracts, Marcia steadily grew her business. Over time, her company also became the nation's largest mover of manufactured homes.

During the 1980 recession, which hit her industry hard, Marcia avoided draconian staff cuts by reducing costs, watching cash flow, and asking all employees to make small sacrifices like taking one day per month off without pay. Meanwhile, the sales team searched for new sources of revenue, and the management team streamlined processes. The family atmosphere that Marcia had developed proved to be a strength that carried her business through the recession. It even prompted employees with resources to take additional days off without pay so that their struggling co-workers wouldn't have to be furloughed. Thus, when the economy rebounded, Bennett Trucking was poised to take more market share and expanded to include multiple trucking companies doing all kinds of transportation.

Today the "Bennett Family of Businesses" consists of 14 companies, boasts 3,200 drivers and owner-operators, and has nearly 400 offices – some outside the United States too. Marcia's "driver retention rates are the envy of the industry." The company's estimated annual revenue as of 2020 was $693 million - with no signs of slowing down.

Entrepreneurship is the pathway to achieving one's dreams. Entrepreneurs want to see their venture flourish into a highly profitable and sustainable business. However, success is hardly ever a straight line, and entrepreneurs need to be prepared for various obstacles that may come their way. To remain relevant and profitable, entrepreneurs must be growth-ready by developing contingency plans, diversifying revenue streams, and creating and monitoring **Key Performance Indicators** (KPIs).

As the global pandemic taught us, disaster planning is a necessity. Entrepreneurs need to develop contingency plans to face unforeseen events such as disasters, economic crises, and pandemics like COVID-19.

A **contingency plan** is a blueprint that outlines how a business will continue to operate during challenging times. It can include strategies such as having a rainy-day fund, identifying, and mitigating potential risks ahead of time, and creating an emergency response team to manage the crisis. A business operating effectively during difficult times can better maintain its customer base, reputation, and profitability.

A business operating effectively during difficult times can better maintain its customer base, reputation, and profitability.

Another business risk mitigation approach is **diversifying revenue streams**. This is a proven way for businesses to ensure continued growth. Popular choices include introducing new products, expanding services into other markets, and developing multiple business models (i.e., online and brick-and-mortar). Diversity in revenue streams ensures that entrepreneurs are not overly dependent on a single product or service to sustain them, thereby reducing risk.

Diversifying revenue streams and reviewing the customer mix of your business is essential for sustained growth. By having multiple revenue streams, your business can minimize its reliance on a single product or service. This will reduce the risk of revenue loss if there is a decrease in demand for that product or service.

By having a diverse customer base, you reduce reliance on a single customer or a specific type of customer. This lessens the impact on revenue in case they decide to switch to a competitor or stop buying altogether. How many times have we heard of a business suffering because it 'lost its largest customer' or their longest standing customer terminated? A diverse portfolio of clientele and regular monitoring of your customer mix can mitigate that risk.

Diversification can enhance the products and services of your business, increasing overall competitiveness in the market. Your business will be able to offer a more comprehensive range of products and services, providing more value to your customers. Diversifying both revenue streams and reviewing the customer mix can help mitigate risks, increase revenue, and expand the business's offerings, all of which are essential for growth in a competitive market.

As Peter Drucker said, "You can't manage what you can't measure." Entrepreneurs must create and monitor Key Performance Indicators (KPIs) to measure the effectiveness and progress of their growth strategies. KPIs are a set of metrics that help entrepreneurs monitor their business performance and track its progress over time. KPIs include customer satisfaction rates, sales growth, and employee turnover rates. By regularly measuring KPIs, entrepreneurs can quickly identify what works and what doesn't, allowing them to make necessary adjustments to their growth strategies. For help identifying what KPI's you should measure for your specific business, visit JackiePTaylor.com.

Setting up KPIs (Key Performance Indicators) for a emerging business can be a valuable tool for tracking progress, making informed decisions, and achieving business objectives. Here are some steps a business owner can follow to create KPIs for their business:

1. **Understand your business goals** - Business owners must understand their goals before creating KPIs. What objectives do they want to achieve? What metrics are essential for their business's success? For instance, a retailer may want to increase sales, reduce inventory costs, or improve customer satisfaction.
2. **Identify specific areas to measure** - Once business owners understand their goals, they must identify specific areas to measure, such as sales, marketing, operations, customer service, or other relevant areas.
3. **Choose relevant KPIs** - Business owners must choose relevant KPIs to track their progress after identifying areas to measure. For example, a retail store may use KPIs such as sales revenue, profit margins, inventory turnover, customer satisfaction, etc.
4. **Use a balanced scorecard** - Business owners should incorporate a balanced scorecard approach, which includes financial and non-financial KPIs. A balanced scorecard provides a comprehensive view of the business's health and enables owners to identify potential issues quickly.
5. **Set specific targets** - Setting clear targets for each KPI helps business owners determine if they are progressing towards their goals. Owners can

target specific values for KPIs and track their progress regularly.

6. **Track and analyze data** – Business owners must track and analyze data regularly to gain insights into their business's performance. They must update their KPIs periodically, review trends, and look for areas to improve.
7. **Take corrective actions** – If business owners identify an area needing improvement, they must take corrective actions to meet their targets. Continuously improving KPIs is essential for making informed decisions and achieving business goals.

Setting up KPIs requires a strategic approach and a commitment to tracking and analyzing data. Entrepreneurs must be growth-ready to build sustainable and thriving businesses.

Diversifying revenue streams, developing contingency plans, and establishing a system of KPIs will ensure entrepreneurs are well-positioned to cope with changes and challenges in their milieu. By being proactive and forward-thinking, entrepreneurs can take concrete steps to set themselves up for success.

Take the time to work ON your business and not just IN your business

All the business readiness insights provided speak to the importance of a founder taking the time to work on the business. Entrepreneurs play a vital role in any economy: they are the driving force behind job creation, economic growth, and innovation. However, for entrepreneurs to succeed and make a significant impact, they must take the time to work ON rather than IN their business.

This involves dedicating time to strategize, plan, and implement long-term goals and objectives.

To begin with, entrepreneurs need to allocate adequate time to work on business strategy, planning and innovationto ensure long-term success. According to a study by the Small Business Administration, only about half of small businesses survive past the five-year mark. This is due to poor planning, lack of funding, and ineffective management. To avoid these pitfalls, entrepreneurs must take the time to work on their business and develop a solid business plan that includes market research, financial projections, and strategies for growth and sustainability.

One example of a successful entrepreneur who dedicated time to working on her business is Sara Blakely, founder of Spanx. Blakely spent two years researching and developing her product before launching it in 2000. She took the time to build a strong brand, secure funding, and create a marketing strategy. Today, Spanx is a global brand worth over $1 billion. Blakely's success is a testament to the importance of entrepreneurs taking the time to work strategically on their businesses.

Another reason entrepreneurs must work on their businesses is to stay competitive in an ever-changing market. The business landscape constantly evolves, and entrepreneurs must adapt to new technologies and consumer trends. By dedicating time to work on their business, entrepreneurs can stay ahead of the curve and remain relevant in their industry.

According to a report by McKinsey, companies that prioritize innovation and stay ahead of the competition are more likely to achieve sustainable growth. By taking the time to work on their business, entrepreneurs can develop innovative products and services that meet the needs of their customers and differentiate themselves from their competitors.

Companies that prioritize innovation and stay ahead of the competition are more likely to achieve sustainable growth. By taking the time to work on their business, entrepreneurs can develop innovative products and services that meet the needs of their customers and differentiate themselves from their competitors.

The importance of entrepreneurs taking the time to work on their businesses cannot be overstated. By doing so, they can develop a solid business plan (a living document that should be regularly revisited), stay competitive, and achieve sustainable growth. As demonstrated by the success of entrepreneurs like Sara Blakely, dedicating time to work on their businesses is essential for long-term success. With the right approach and mindset, entrepreneurs can build successful companies that positively impact their communities and the economy.

How much time should you spend working ON your business?

First, working on your business isn't something that should cease once you launch. Although pre-planning is essential, business strategy and innovation should occur throughout the lifetime of your enterprise.

According to a survey conducted by the Kauffman Foundation, most successful entrepreneurs spend about 40% of their workweek on developing and executing business strategies. This translates to about 24 hours per week or 4.8 hours per day.

Another survey by The Alternative Board (TAB) found that business owners spend an average of 21% of their time on planning and strategy. However, high-performing businesses spend significantly more time on strategy, with the top-performing companies devoting up to 40% of their time to strategic planning.

Most experts recommend that entrepreneurs spend 20-40% of their time on business strategy, depending on their needs and growth stage. However, it's important to note that every business is unique. The time spent on strategy will depend on various factors, such as size, industry, and market trends.

Think about your typical work week or your typical month. How much time do you currently spend on planning and strategy? Are you spending just enough, not enough, or too much time?

____

____

____

____

____

____

NOTES

-CHAPTER 2-

BOOST! YOUR MARKETING AND BRANDING

MARKETING AND BRANDING ARE CRUCIAL for any business, regardless of size or resources. However, emerging businesses and historically under-resourced companies have faced significant challenges in marketing and branding. They typically have limited resources, smaller budgets, and fewer staff members to allocate to the marketing and branding efforts. As a result, it can be difficult for these businesses to develop an effective marketing strategy, create a strong brand identity, and reach their target audience effectively.

Under-resourced businesses must adopt a strategic approach to succeed in marketing and branding. They must create a comprehensive plan outlining their marketing goals, target audience, budget, and tactics to reach and engage their audience. This plan should also include an analysis of competitors, identifying their strengths and weaknesses and areas where they can differentiate themselves from the competition. Although this is a key exercise for all businesses, it is especially important for under-resourced businesses who have to be more judicious and deliberate about their spend.

Developing a solid brand identity is one of the most critical aspects of a successful marketing and branding plan. This involves creating a consistent image and message that resonates with the target audience. Smaller businesses can differentiate themselves by focusing on their unique selling points and values that differentiate them from their competitors.

What differentiates your business?

____

____

____

____

____

____

Another essential factor in marketing and branding is leveraging social media and other digital channels. These platforms offer cost-effective ways for under-resourced businesses to reach their target audience, build relationships, and promote their products and services. Social media platforms such as Tik Tok, Facebook, Instagram, LinkedIn, and Twitter can help businesses reach new customers organically and amplify their messages through influencers and paid advertising.

Under-resourced businesses should utilize tools that can automate tasks and provide analytics and insights to measure their marketing impact to make the most of social media and other digital marketing channels. They should also analyze consumer trends, take advantage of strategic partnerships, and collaborate with influencers and other businesses in their industry.

Marketing and branding are essential for any business, big or small. Historically under-resourced companies face significant challenges in developing an effective marketing strategy, creating a strong brand identity, and reaching their target audience. To overcome these challenges, they need to adopt a strategic approach, focus on their unique selling points, leverage digital channels, and collaborate with partners in the industry. By doing so, under-resourced businesses can succeed in marketing and branding their products and services and achieve their business objectives.

Historically under-resourced companies face significant challenges in developing an effective marketing strategy, creating a strong brand identity, and reaching their target audience. To overcome these challenges, they need to adopt a strategic approach, focus on their unique selling points, leverage digital channels, and collaborate with partners in the industry.

I suggest several marketing strategies for under-resourced businesses looking to grow

1. **Understand Your Customers –** Understanding who your customers are and what they need is essential. Take the time to research their needs and preferences and create a personalized experience based on that. So many businesses play it by ear, which is a surefire way to derail your exponential growth plans.
2. **Optimize Your Web Pages –** Create web pages that are clear, easy to navigate, and visually appealing. Make sure the content is concise and relevant, and the navigation intuitive. Do not rely on Facebook or individual social media pages to substitute your web page. Snag a URL(custom website address), and establish a strong web presence.

3. **Leverage Automation** – Automation can help streamline processes and make them easier for customers. This can include setting up automated emails, personalized product recommendations, and purchase tracking.
4. **Use Mobile Technologies** – Mobile technologies allow customers to access products and services when and where they need them. Make sure your digital experience is optimized for mobile and tablet usage.
5. **Offer Multiple Payment Options** – Make sure your customers can pay for their purchases in the most convenient way. Offer multiple payment options like credit cards, digital wallets, and payment systems like PayPal. Cash is no longer king when it comes to consumer pay practices.
6. **Personalize Your Approach** – Get to know your customers and contact them with personalized communications. Send segmented emails when customers have abandoned their carts or informative blog posts when purchasing a particular product.
7. **Utilize Customer Reviews** – Reviews are a powerful tool that can help build trust and increase customer engagement. Consider adding customer reviews to your website and use them as an opportunity to improve your customer experience.
8. **Integrate Social Media** – Social media can be a powerful tool for engaging customers and building relationships. Consider integrating popular social media platforms into your digital experience and

keep track of customer feedback and questions. Use Google My Business and Google Analytics.

Consumers now expect personalized experiences, and marketers can achieve this by utilizing data to understand preferences. In the age of digital marketing, consumers have grown accustomed to personalized experiences. This means that consumers expect the brands they interact with to understand their preferences and offer products and services that align with their needs. For example, if a customer frequently buys organic and natural products, they expect to receive suggestions for similar products based on this preference.

Consumers now expect personalized experiences, and marketers can achieve this by utilizing data to understand preferences.

To meet this expectation, marketers can utilize the vast amount of data available to gain insights into consumer behavior and preferences. These insights can be used to create targeted marketing campaigns that resonate with specific segments of the consumer base. By leveraging data, marketers can craft messaging and advertising that speaks directly to a consumer's interests, increasing the chances of conversion.

For example, a clothing retailer may collect data on a customer's purchase history, browsing behavior, and demographics to better understand their interests and preferences. This information can then be used to create a personalized email campaign that suggests clothing items similar to what the customer has purchased or viewed online. By providing personalized recommendations, the retailer can increase the likelihood of a purchase and improve customer retention.

Overall, personalized experiences are now table stakes in the marketing world, and leveraging data is one of the key ways marketers can achieve this. By understanding consumer preferences and behaviors, emerging business owners like yourself can create messaging and products that resonate with your audience, building stronger relationships and driving revenue.

Social media has transformed marketing, creating opportunities for engagement with customers. Social media has revolutionized how businesses market their products and services, providing new opportunities for customer engagement. In the past, traditional marketing methods such as print advertisements, flyers, billboards, and television commercials were often one-way communication channels, with businesses shouting their message to potential customers without receiving any feedback. However, social media has allowed companies to interact in a more personal and engaging way with their audience.

Social media platforms such as Facebook, Tik Tok, Instagram, Twitter, and LinkedIn provide a two-way communication channel where businesses can share their message with their followers, engage with them, and receive feedback. This has opened up new avenues for businesses to create lasting customer relationships, increasing brand awareness and loyalty.

Moreover, social media has allowed businesses to target specific demographics, reaching a wider audience and increasing their chances of converting potential customers into paying ones. The ability to analyze social media data and user behavior means that businesses can tailor their marketing messages to the needs and preferences of their target audience. As a result, companies can deliver personalized messages to their customers, increasing the relevance and impact of their campaigns. This represents an opportunity for you as the business owner!

The benefits of social media marketing are clear, and companies that leverage this powerful tool will undoubtedly be able to build stronger relationships with their customers and increase their market share in the long term.

Artificial intelligence and automation technologies enable businesses to gain insights and better manage campaigns. These cutting-edge technologies are enhancing the ability of companies to gain insights and make informed decisions about their campaigns.

AI-enabled tools can now analyze large volumes of data and help businesses identify significant patterns and trends that were previously difficult to detect. This new level of analysis allows companies to make informed decisions about which campaigns are working and which need to be modified. Most importantly, you don't have to be a techie to take advantage of these tools.

Automation technologies are also playing a significant role in streamlining campaign management processes. Businesses can minimize errors and improve efficiencies by automating ad creation and distribution tasks. This adds the benefit of reducing employees' workload, freeing up valuable resources that can be redirected towards higher-value tasks.

AI is currently being used in a number of ways to assist emerging business owners. Here are a few examples:

- AI-based tools can assist in market research by providing insights into customer needs, preferences, and expectations, allowing business owners to make informed decisions regarding their products and services.
- AI-powered chatbots can provide real-time customer support, freeing up time for employees to concentrate on other duties.
- AI can aid in making data-driven decisions regarding marketing and advertising strategies, offering insights into target audiences, developing content, and keeping track of trends.
- AI-powered social media scheduling and analysis tools can streamline social media management tasks such as scheduling posts, analyzing performance, and developing targeted campaigns.
- AI can be used to automate repetitive and time-consuming tasks such as data entry and invoice management, allowing employees to focus on critical strategic tasks.
- AI can analyze customer data to provide a personalized experience by delivering tailored recommendations and promotions.
- AI algorithms can analyze sales data to forecast future sales, helping emerging businesses make informed decisions regarding inventory management and investments.

Emerging business owners can benefit from these innovative AI tools to increase efficiency and customer satisfaction while achieving their business goals.

Together, AI and automation technologies are allowing businesses to more effectively and efficiently manage their campaigns, enabling them to allocate resources more effectively and achieve better results. As these technologies evolve, companies that embrace them will be best positioned to thrive in the ever-changing digital landscape.

To meet customers' expectations, founders should create immersive digital experiences using the latest technologies and platforms available. As more businesses take advantage of these capabilities, they become less differentiating. Be an early adopter so you can reap the benefits before the market becomes too saturated.

NOTES

-CHAPTER 3-

BOOST! YOUR PEOPLE RESOURCES

THE INCREASINGLY COMPETITIVE MARKET IS presenting many challenges to emerging businesses. As you grow, you'll compete with larger organizations, so you must make the most of limited resources while finding creative ways to remain competitive. One of the most important resources to any organization, small or large, is its workforce. Unfortunately, emerging businesses often face unique workforce challenges that can be difficult to overcome.

One of the most common challenges emerging businesses face is the recruiting, hiring, and retaining of employees. Emerging businesses often lack the resources and financial incentives that larger organizations can offer, which makes it difficult to compete for the best talent. Furthermore, talent shortages and high employee turnover can pressure emerging businesses, resulting in difficulty staffing their operations. Emerging businesses should focus on defining and promoting their culture, taking an active role in their local communities, and finding creative ways to offer competitive benefits to overcome this challenge.

> ***Emerging** businesses often lack the resources and financial incentives that larger organizations can offer, which makes it difficult to compete for the best talent.*

Another common challenge for emerging businesses is managing employee performance

Many emerging business owners neglect this very important aspect. They may hire family or friends (or framily-friends who are as close as family), which makes formal reviewing processes somewhat awkward. This is why training and structure are so necessary. You may lack the resources to garner sufficient employee feedback and also lack resources to provide the professional development training that your team needs. In turn, this can lead to reduced job satisfaction, lack of motivation, and poor overall performance. Emerging businesses must invest in training programs and create a culture of continuous feedback to counteract this issue. Additionally, they can create performance review systems that are transparent and easy to understand, ensuring that employees are held accountable for their work.

Yet another workforce challenge faced by emerging businesses is managing employee compensation. A limited budget can make offering fair wages and benefits difficult, especially when competing with larger organizations. Yet growing companies can create flexible compensation packages that include equity (for select roles), bonuses, and other incentives. Furthermore, they should focus on creating a culture of appreciation and recognition. Acknowledging each employee's contributions can create an environment of mutual respect and appreciation that will increase job satisfaction and loyalty. Flexible work arrangements can also sweeten the comp package/offer.

Emerging businesses face workforce challenges similar to larger organizations but are constrained due to their limited resources. They must work to find creative ways to recruit, hire, and retain employees, manage performance, and offer competitive compensation packages. With the right approach, emerging businesses can overcome these issues and create a productive and successful workforce.

Battaglia Associates, Inc.

Christine Meyer and her sister, Jennifer Battaglia, worked for years in their family's industrial contracting business. Hoping to break into real estate, they purchased a real estate venture, Battaglia Associates, Inc. (BAI), *from their parents in 2007. Off to a great start, they suddenly hit a brick wall in 2008 when the real estate market stalled. They plowed through, taking on whatever jobs they could find, and managed to keep the business afloat. In 2015, they got their break, completing two key projects, a substation security installation and work for a fencing company. "We ended up doing about $2 million in 2015...In 2016, we got nine of those projects, and by 2017 it kept growing and got crazy."*

Today Battaglia Associates Inc., *a certified* Women's Business Enterprise (WBE), *is an industry-leading general contractor providing procurement construction, maintenance, and repair services in the heavy commercial, industrial and energy markets. The company has completed projects in five states, offering a broad range of specialty services—from U.L.-certified panel fabrication and security infrastructure installation to structured cabling and substation construction and maintenance.*

The secret to their success: *Christine and Jennifer credit much of their success to having the right team members. "I surround myself with the best people,"* Christine *says. "My contracts manager is a rock star; my sister takes care of the back end and keeps everybody happy. I have a great division manager; he knows it all. I'm proud of all the people I work with and how far we've come together because it's tough to be a woman in construction."* BAI *is not only woman-owned; its team comprises quite a few women, bringing new skills and insight to the workplace while making this company unique to this male-dominated industry. "We bid and manage every project with a team approach.You can speak with any member of our team, and they will know details on most of our projects because we are all invested in the success of the company.... This sense of community is central to what* BAI *does,"* Christine *continues: "There is a pride that we all have watching this company grow, knowing that every person on the team has been crucial in making that happen."*

BAI *is realistic. Besides capitalizing on their team's strengths, they recognize limitations and proactively connect with available business organizations to fill those gaps.* Thus, Battaglia *has drawn on resources like the* Maryland Washington Minority Companies Association, *the* Women's Business Enterprise National Council, *and the* Women Presidents' Organization (WPO) *to enhance their capabilities.* Consequently, BAI *has become the fifth fastest-growing woman-owned/ led company.*

Too many emerging business owners get so caught up in everyday operations, like marketing and sales, that their workforce becomes no more than an afterthought. This is the wrong approach. Your workforce is one of your greatest growth assets. Cultivating the right team is your 'secret sauce' to growing your business.

Today's workplace has changed dramatically over the past few decades. Business owners who don't bother to address these changes put themselves at a distinct disadvantage.

One significant change involves the workforce. "...[Employees] hardly ever remain with one company for their entire career." As a result, there is a much faster turnover of talent and fewer loyal, experienced employees who can keep the company on track. Owen Sweeney notes, however, that this "... doesn't mean that businesses should stop focusing on developing their future leaders from within." As the Digital and Social Content Manager for Sage Canada, Sweeney speaks from experience. He offers several practical suggestions to help business owners fine-tune their workforce and develop leaders and motivators from within their company.

As a company begins to grow, the first impulse of many owners is to find new hires to supplement their workforce. There are circumstances when this is the smart thing to do. However, Sweeney makes a good point: "Leaders grown from within an organization will be positioned for success in their new roles because they're familiar with organizational challenges or growth areas compared to a person joining the organization for the first time."

Moreover, training new hires is an added expense. It is much more cost-effective to provide skills training to existing employees. Furthermore, you want your people to aspire to gain new skills and see themselves as valuable assets to your business.

Below are Sweeney's guidelines for training and motivating your workforce:

1. *Identify and act on areas where up-skilling could be beneficial.*
2. *Establish consistent communication and goal setting.*
3. *Show appreciation.*
4. *Build and grow positive relationships.*
5. *Offer flexible and remote working.*
6. *Boost employee wellbeing.*

Sometimes it makes sense to hire new employees, but determining exactly *when* to hire keeps emerging business owners up at night. Here are five indicators that it may be time to hire more workers:

1. Spending significant time on non-crucial activities and tasks
2. The quality of customer service is deteriorating
3. You have contractors that have been with you long term and their loss would be detrimental
4. You will be taking on new, significant business and need additional capacity
5. Noticing that the current staff is visibly overwhelmed with work

Even so, it is still a matter of degree. *How much* valuable time is being lost? Are your employees struggling to keep up? Is your staff falling behind or seriously exhausted? Let your instincts guide you before you run to Indeed.com, or consider whether outsourcing might fix the problem.

I provide a tool to my founder mentees trying to determine their workforce needs.. **The three D's** - Do, Delegate, Dedicate.

DO – Should you just do it yourself?

Deciding whether to delegate a particular task to one of your employees, outsource it, hire someone new, or just do it yourself needs to be an objective decision rather than an emotional one.

There is a good reason I mention this. If you let it, being an emerging business owner tends to force you into a mindset that can sabotage your efforts to grow. Out of necessity, you have to wear many hats. You constantly move between departments —accounting, production, marketing, etc. Hey, this is your baby. You want to ensure that every aspect of your business runs smoothly, so you are *very* hands-on. You may delegate some tasks, but you carry most of the burden on your shoulders.

Most emerging business owners don't even realize how much they do. Have you ever put a monetary value on your time and your work? How much would it cost for you to outsource everything you do for your business?

Just for fun, try the following exercise to see what percentage of your time you spend on the various aspects of your business:

1. Make a list of everything you do each week (or every two weeks) to run your business. Include what

you do in accounting, manufacturing, marketing, sales, direct contact with clients, contracts and legal work, travel, customer service, overseeing your employees, HR, etc.

2. Assign a % to each item to show how much time you spend on them. Do you have any time left over?
3. Now ask yourself, what % of time do I spend being a visionary for my business? In other words, as the owner, CEO, or president, what do you want next for your company? Where do you see your company five or ten years down the road? How successful do you want it to be?

DELEGATE what you can – Identify another resource inside your business to own and complete the tasks in this category. The time you spend picturing where your business is going adds the most value – more than everything else you do to keep your business running. If you don't give yourself enough time to dream, you are doing yourself, your business, and your customers a disservice. It's okay to dream a little. Dreaming a lot about your business and what it can become is okay. **You are not wasting time by dreaming —you are *harnessing* it for the future!**

But you can't achieve that dream by yourself. The engine of your business is your workforce. Your employees put your plan into action! If you instill that dream into your people and teach them your growth mindset, your business will be unstoppable!

DEDICATE to an outside vendor who will own it – Commonly referred to as outsourcing. Outsourcing specific tasks or jobs can effectively and economically expand your workforce without breaking the bank. Think about the costs of bringing on even one new employee. You have to pay for training, which often means pulling one of your supervisors from what they usually do to train the new individual. You also have to pay toward health and life insurance, pension, etc., as well as their paychecks and payroll taxes.

With outsourcing, you are dealing with a 3rd party vendor, not employees or contractors. This means that you only owe them for the work they do. You do not need to cover the additional costs of having another employee or provide direct oversight.

Outsourcing is flexible: you can outsource one task or a set of tasks, pay by the project or the hour, and have the person work full-time or part-time, on-site or remotely.

James Bucki, in his article, "Top Outsourcing Advantages,"[6] explains the benefits of Outsourcing. He says that outsourcing enables you to:

- Focus on core tasks
- Lower costs
- Promote growth
- Maintain operational control
- Offer staffing flexibility
- Provide continuity and risk management
- Develop internal staff

Don't rush this process. The key to successful growth is putting together the right team to handle the stage of development your business is in. This means accepting your limitations and those of your current workforce. It means being receptive to the potential of each of your employees and equipping and motivating them. Finally, it means using your entrepreneurial instincts to know when and how much capital to invest in bringing in additional talent when needed.

NOTES

-CHAPTER 4-

BOOST! YOUR ENERGY

When Life Starts 'Lifing'

LIVING IN A POST-PANDEMIC WORLD, we can all attest that sometimes, despite our best plans, the most unexpected things happen. We must be prepared to pivot. We all experience the hardships of life, and entrepreneurs are not exempt. In fact, some studies say the opposite.

Several studies have suggested that entrepreneurs are more likely to experience mental health challenges than people who are not self-employed. A 2015 study conducted by the University of California San Francisco found that entrepreneurs were more likely to report symptoms of ADHD, bipolar disorder, and depression compared to the general population.

Similarly, a 2020 study conducted by the National Institute of Mental Health found that emerging business owners and entrepreneurs were more likely to experience symptoms of depression, anxiety, and stress compared to workers who were not self-employed.

2020 study conducted by the National Institute of Mental Health found that emerging business owners and entrepreneurs were more likely to experience symptoms of depression, anxiety, and stress compared to workers who were not self-employed.

The reasons behind this trend are complex and multifaceted. Entrepreneurship is known for its high stress, uncertainty, and risk-taking levels, which can contribute to mental health challenges. Entrepreneurial work also tends to be more isolating. Due to stigma, lack of time, or financial constraints, entrepreneurs may be less likely to seek help for their mental health concerns.

Overall, the prevalence of mental health diagnoses among entrepreneurs and emerging business owners highlights this group's need for more support and resources. Such resources include counseling services, mentorship programs, and access to affordable healthcare. By promoting the mental health and wellbeing of entrepreneurs and emerging business owners, society can help unlock innovation's full potential and new business creation.

As an emerging business owner, managing and boosting your energy levels is crucial to stay motivated, productive, and successful in your business endeavors. In today's fast-paced world, it is easy to get caught up in the hustle and bustle of running a business and neglect the importance of taking care of yourself. However, it is essential to remember that as a business founder, your health and wellbeing are crucial to your overall success. Neglecting your energy levels can lead to burnout, exhaustion, and decreased productivity, ultimately harming your business. Therefore, protecting your energy as a business founder should be a priority because, as the age-old adage goes, 'health is wealth.'

As an ***emerging*** *business owner, managing and boosting your energy levels is crucial to stay motivated, productive, and successful in your business endeavors. In today's fast-paced world, it is easy to get caught up in the hustle and bustle of running a business and neglect the importance of taking care of yourself.*

One of the most significant risks of neglecting your energy levels and experiencing burnout is that it can harm your business's overall productivity and success. In fact, according to a study by the Harvard Business Review, employee burnout can lead to up to 60% more errors and a 50% increase in turnover rates. These statistics are alarming, especially considering that business owners often wear many hats and are responsible for many aspects of their businesses. As a result, emerging business owners who neglect their energy levels are likely to experience similar productivity declines and adverse outcomes.

One notable example of an entrepreneur who experienced burnout and suffered the consequences is Arianna Huffington, founder of the Huffington Post. Huffington worked long hours, often going without sleep for extended periods, and experienced burnout in 2007. Her burnout led to a broken cheekbone and reevaluating her lifestyle and priorities. In response, Huffington made changes such as getting more sleep, exercising, and meditating, which improved her overall health and helped her become a better leader for her business.

Another example is Emily Weiss, founder of the beauty brand Glossier. Weiss admitted that she initially ignored her energy levels and worked long hours, neglecting her sleep and health. However, after experiencing burnout, she realized she needed to prioritize her health and wellbeing to achieve her goals. By taking care of herself and prioritizing her energy levels, Weiss was able to build a successful company that has since been valued at over $1 billion.

You can take several steps to protect your energy levels as a emerging business founder.

First, make sure to prioritize getting enough sleep each night. Sleep is essential for restoring your energy levels and overall health. Additionally, exercise regularly, eat a nutritious diet, and take breaks throughout the day to avoid burnout. Finally, make sure to disconnect from work, when possible, whether that means taking a vacation or simply setting boundaries around when you check your email. Six strategies are outlined in greater detail later in this chapter. Use this checklist to stay on track.

Protecting your energy levels as a emerging business founder is vital to your success. Neglecting your energy levels can lead to burnout, exhaustion, and decreased productivity, ultimately harming your business. Taking care of yourself by prioritizing sleep, exercise, and breaks throughout the day can help you maintain your energy levels and become a better leader for your business. Remember, as the age-old adage goes, "Health is wealth."

Energy is the driving force behind business success. It is the resource that fuels your motivation, productivity, and creativity. Without enough energy, your ability to innovate, problem-solve and make sound decisions can be significantly diminished. Moreover, good health is vital for business success.

According to a study by the Small Business Administration (SBA), entrepreneurs with better health were more likely to have higher revenue growth and be more successful in their businesses.

According to a study by the Small Business Administration (SBA), entrepreneurs with better health were more likely to have higher revenue growth and be more successful in their businesses.

Factors Affecting Energy Levels

Several factors can influence your energy levels. Work-life balance, sleep, nutrition, physical activity, and stress management are crucial in determining your energy levels. Neglecting any of these factors can significantly decrease your energy levels and ultimately result in burnout and exhaustion.

Energy levels are an essential factor in the lives of business owners. They are the driving force that keeps them motivated and passionate about their work. However, maintaining high energy levels can be challenging, particularly for today's business owners. Several factors affect energy levels, including stress, burnout, lifestyle habits, and work environments.

One of the most significant factors affecting energy levels is burnout. According to a recent study, entrepreneurs experience burnout at rates higher than the general population. The study found that 45% of entrepreneurs reported feeling burnt out at least once in their careers. Furthermore, 26% of entrepreneurs said they experience burnout frequently, and 3% reported experiencing it all the time.

According to a recent study, entrepreneurs experience burnout at rates higher than the general population. The study found that 45% of entrepreneurs reported feeling burnt out at least once in their careers. Furthermore, 26% of entrepreneurs said they experience burnout frequently, and 3% reported experiencing it all the time.

There are several reasons why entrepreneurs experience burnout. Firstly, they tend to work long hours and have a high workload, which can lead to fatigue and exhaustion. Secondly, entrepreneurs often face significant stress and pressure, particularly during the early stages of their business. Thirdly, entrepreneurs may experience a lack of support and resources, which can cause them to feel overwhelmed and discouraged.

Another significant factor affecting energy levels is lifestyle habits. Business owners who lead unhealthy lifestyles, such as a lack of sleep, poor diets, and inadequate exercise, are likely to experience low energy levels. Studies have shown that a healthy lifestyle, including regular exercise, a balanced diet, and sufficient sleep, can significantly improve energy levels.

Work environments can also play a significant role in energy levels. Business owners who work in stressful and unproductive environments may experience low energy levels. If the business owner's energy is depleted, it can CREATE a toxic, stressful work environment. On the other hand, those who work in supportive and collaborative environments may experience higher energy levels.

It can't be emphasized enough that good to excellent energy levels are essential for business owners. Burnout, lifestyle habits, and work environments are some of the significant factors that affect energy levels. With the high rates of burnout among entrepreneurs, it is essential to take steps to prevent burnout and maintain high energy levels. Business owners should prioritize their health, lead a healthy lifestyle, and create a supportive work environment to keep their energy levels and achieve success.

Strategies for Boosting and Managing Energy Levels

As an emerging business owner, the following strategies can help you to manage and boost your energy levels. Refer to the checklist below to stay on track.

- **Prioritize self-care**: Setting aside time for self-care activities such as meditation, exercise, reading, and hobbies is crucial for replenishing your energy levels.
- **Time management techniques**: Use productivity tools such as calendars, to-do lists, and project management software to manage your time effectively and free up mental space.
- **Mindfulness practices**: Mindfulness practices such as deep breathing or yoga can help to reduce stress and boost energy levels.
- **Healthy lifestyle habits**: A nutritious diet, getting enough exercise and sleep, and avoiding unhealthy habits such as smoking or excessive drinking can help to boost energy levels.

- **Delegation to manage workload**: Delegating tasks to others and outsourcing specific projects can free up your time and energy, allowing you to focus on high-priority tasks.
- **SLEEP!** So often, business owners neglect their sleep. Sleep is medicine. Sleep is essential. There are so many instances where the answer is to drink more water and get more sleep!

There are consequences to a lack of energy management

Ignoring poor energy management and signs of burnout in entrepreneurs can severely affect their health, productivity, and overall business success. Some of the consequences are:

1. **Poor Health –** Ignoring burnout and poor energy management can lead to mental and physical health problems. According to a study by the American Psychological Association, chronic stress can lead to anxiety, depression, and cardiovascular disease.
2. **Decreased Productivity** – Burned-out entrepreneurs may experience decreased productivity and creativity, leading to missed deadlines and reduced quality of work.
3. **Increased Staff Turnover** – Burnout can lead to a higher business turnover rate. Employees may leave due to a lack of leadership and vision.
4. **Financial Loss** – Poor energy management can lead to financial loss as entrepreneurs may make poor decisions, miss opportunities, or fail to meet business goals.

NOTES

NOTES

-CHAPTER 5-

BOOST! INNOVATION & TECHNOLOGY

TECHNOLOGY IS INDEED THE GREAT accelerator. Many businesses leverage emerging technologies to catapult their revenue and operations. If you are truly ready for your business to grow and move to the next level, read on.

Innovation and technology have been the primary drivers of the growth and scaling of businesses for a while now. We all know emerging enterprises are vital to the economy, contributing significantly to job creation, economic growth, and innovation.

Innovation refers to the process of creating something new or making improvements to an existing product or service.

Technology includes the tools, equipment, and techniques used to facilitate innovation.

Innovation refers to the process of creating something new or making improvements to an existing product or service.
Technology includes the tools, equipment, and techniques used to facilitate innovation.

One of the ways innovation and technology drive the growth and scaling of emerging businesses is through adopting new business models. Innovative business models enable emerging businesses to capitalize on emerging trends, improve operations, and reach new markets.

Examples of innovative business models include subscription-based models and platforms that allow businesses to provide goods and services directly to consumers. Through these models, companies can innovate their products and services, making them more attractive to consumers and increasing their customer base.

Questions to Ask Yourself

Are you currently leveraging technology in your business? To get your juices flowing, I've added a few examples below of areas where you can consider technology to scale your business. Check where you may currently be leveraging technology. Add any we may not have mentioned.

- ☐ Payroll
- ☐ Accounts Receivable/ Accounts Payable
- ☐ Training and onboarding Employees or contractors
- ☐ Online training for your customers or prospects
- ☐ Translating your expertise or activities to digital or automating
- ☐ Public Relations (press release generation and pitching)
- ☐ Sales Outreach
- ☐ Inventory Management
- ☐ Customer Relationship Management & Sentiments

____

____

____

____

Adopting emerging technologies is another way that emerging businesses can scale and grow

Although I am a proponent of leveraging emerging technologies to scale your business, I caution you to pace yourself. Some very robust enterprise-level solutions in the market may be overkill for your needs - akin to using a shotgun to kill a flea. Take your time and assess your needs against the capabilities of the technologies that you're considering.

Emerging technologies, such as artificial intelligence, blockchain, and the Internet of Things, are transforming the business landscape. Businesses that adopt them can gain a competitive advantage.

Businesses can use artificial intelligence to improve customer service, automate routine tasks, and analyze customer data to understand consumer behavior better. By doing so, companies can identify new opportunities to increase revenue, boost efficiency, and reduce costs.

Emerging businesses can also leverage technology to develop new products or services. Technology has made it easier and less expensive for companies to create and test new products and services. Emerging businesses can use online platforms for crowdsourcing consumer ideas, collaborate with other companies or designers, and use 3D printing to create prototypes quickly and inexpensively. Emerging businesses can also use technology to customize products or services to fit customers' specific needs, thus improving customer satisfaction and loyalty.

Innovation and technology can also help emerging businesses to reach new markets. Digital marketing tools like social media, search engine optimization, and email marketing enable emerging businesses to reach a wider audience and build brand awareness. This can help emerging businesses to expand their customer base, increase revenue and scale up their operations.

Innovation and technology are fundamental to the growth and scaling of emerging businesses. Emerging businesses that embrace innovative business models adopt emerging technologies and develop new products and services. They can gain a competitive advantage, expand their customer base, and drive revenue growth. Technology has revolutionized every aspect of business. Emerging businesses that recognize this and embrace innovation and technology will thrive in the digital age.

Technology as a complement to your workforce needs

Growing businesses must work to achieve a healthy balance between technology and the output of their workforce. Have you considered what will happen once you expand your business? If your people are already working at close to 100% capacity, one possible multiplier is technology. The technology you use has to be able to multiply their time and effort, for your business to handle an additional load.

The question is, can the technology you currently have handle it, or do you need to upgrade or implement something new?

The question is, can the technology you currently have handle it, or do you need to upgrade or implement something new?

The word 'technology' covers quite a bit of ground—from computer equipment, software, and apps, to the internet and social media, smartphones, and hand-held devices for scanning and quickly gathering data to artificial intelligence and blockchain. Depending on your business type, you are probably already using a number of these.

Emerge

Andrew Leto, a five-year veteran of the U.S. Navy, is the founder and CEO of Emerge, a freight logistics startup in Scottsdale, AZ, that is transforming the industry. Andrew and his brother, Michael, had been in freight transportation since 1999, working at their father's air freight company.

Experts in their field and intimately familiar with the needs of truckers and shipping companies, Andrew and Michael founded GlobalTranz in 2003. GlobalTranz quickly became one of the top 10 U.S. Truckload and LTL brokers, topping a billion dollars in sales. After selling GlobalTranz for more than $400 million, the brothers decided to address a trucking headache that has plagued truckers and shippers alike: the laborious bidding process that every shipper has to go through for each contract. Andrew's idea was to create a freight marketplace platform accessible online to all the parties involved. This new software technology would streamline logistics and get freight to where it needed to be on time and at the lowest possible cost.

Emerge was officially launched in 2017 with Andrew as chairman and Michael as CEO. It sped up critical activities like quote management and analytics.

With its Freight Procurement Platform, shippers and carriers could now view marketplace fluctuations as they happened and adjust their bids and contracts accordingly. It also offered real-time tracking, live support chats, and automated late and repeat shipment scheduling. Above all, it gave them access to over 30,000+ pre-vetted carriers to develop the best combination of price and service. Andrew calls this blend of access and speed 'The Network Effect.'

The company outpaced all expectations. By 2018, over $100M was procured through this platform; the following year, that number zoomed up to over $500M. In 2020, Andrew introduced another platform, the Dynamic RFP (Request for Proposal) Platform, using more advanced software technology. This new program removed two significant limitations shippers had been struggling with: 1. conducting business manually and 2. being limited to only a few carriers at a time. With this new technology, shippers could start developing relationships with as many carriers as needed for each contracted job—all with a few clicks. By 2021, thanks to the Dynamic RFP Platform, the procurement totals grew to over $1B. Today, the run rate procured through the platform is over $6B.

The breathtaking speed of growth that Emerge experienced was the result of creatively applying the newest technology as it became available. Emerge was connected with freight transportation, a high-volume, high-revenue business. However, capitalizing on technology this way can let any size or type of business experience exponential growth and turn problems into potential.

To ensure you aren't missing out on a technology hack that could make all the difference for your company, let's check with Fabrizio Moreira. As a business mentor and entrepreneur, Moreira knows what businesses need to succeed and grow. In his *Lifehack.org* article, 'Seven Ways Technology Makes your Emerging Business Grow Faster,' Moreira points out several areas where today's technology can enable you as a smaller business to compete with larger ones and, with that advantage, quickly grow it.

Here are four that you should know:

1. **Cloud data storage**

One of the best improvements that today's technology gives you is convenient and unlimited data storage with the Cloud. Rather than worrying about backup drives and accidentally losing files, all your data can be set up to automatically back up to the Cloud, which is a secure, highly encrypted online system. This way, your employees and clients can access the data they need from anywhere in the world and even collaborate on the same document.

2. **Productivity Apps**

Every serious business owner can find areas where productivity is sluggish. Old, outdated programs or still doing things by hand cause bottlenecks in everything from sales to accounting and manufacturing. Use the best software packages (see below) and apps you can leverage. This list constantly changes, so visit JackiePTaylor.com for the most up-to-date information. These will save you time and frustration and make your workforce far more efficient (they will be much happier, too!).

Do a little research to see which apps provide what your company needs. Moreira adds, "...many of these apps can be synced with their desktop versions and are completely free or offer a free level of service," so you can easily test them out before committing:

- Slack
- Trello
- Asana
- Podio
- Basecamp

3. **Analytical Tools**

Moreira describes what analytical tools do but does not suggest any particular ones. The world of emerging business is vastly different today than it was just a few decades ago. Technology has completely transformed the business landscape. The internet, social media, and mobile devices give emerging business owners powerful tools to reach new customers and streamline their operations. However, with so many options available, it can be overwhelming for emerging business owners to figure out which analytical tools they can use to optimize their operations and grow their businesses faster.

One of emerging business owners' most important analytical tools is customer relationship management (CRM) software. A CRM system provides businesses with a centralized customer information database, allowing them to track customer interactions and identify engagement opportunities. Companies can create personalized marketing campaigns by analyzing customer data and tailoring their products and services to better fit their customers' needs. CRM systems also often provide insights into customer behavior, allowing businesses to understand how their customers interact with their products and where there might be gaps or areas for improvement.

Another powerful analytical tool for emerging businesses is website analytics. By tracking website traffic and user behavior, companies can gain valuable insights into how visitors interact with their site and identify growth opportunities. Website analytics can provide information on which pages are most popular, which elements on the page are most engaging, and where visitors are dropping off in the conversion process. With this data, businesses can make informed decisions about website changes and marketing strategies to attract customers and increase sales.

Social media analytics is also becoming an increasingly important tool for emerging businesses. With billions of people using social media daily, companies can leverage social platforms to reach new audiences and engage with customers in real time. By analyzing social media analytics data, businesses can track engagement, measure marketing campaigns' success, and identify growth opportunities. In addition, companies can use social listening tools to monitor what customers say about their brand online and react to feedback.

One final analytical tool that emerging businesses can leverage to make their businesses grow faster is data visualization software. By visualizing data, companies can quickly identify patterns and trends that might not be immediately apparent. Data visualization tools can help emerging business owners turn complex data sets into easy-to-interpret charts and graphs, allowing them to make informed decisions based on data-driven insights. Tableau is an example of data visualization software.

Many analytical tools are available to emerging business owners looking to leverage technology to make their businesses grow faster. Many of these tools are industry specific. These tools include CRM software, website analytics, social media analytics, and data visualization software. By analyzing customer data, tracking website traffic and user behavior, monitoring social media engagement, and visualizing complex data sets, emerging business owners can make informed decisions and take targeted actions to accelerate business growth.

4. **Better Marketing Campaigns**

Digital marketing campaigns allow businesses to target specific target markets, get immediate results, test different approaches, and find out how the campaign is doing even while the campaign is ongoing. They offer a higher ROI than more traditional forms of advertising do. What emerging businesses like most about this type of marketing is that it levels the playing field when competing against bigger businesses.

Below are some additional areas where I have found that technology can measurably speed up your company's growth and boost profits:

1. **Everyday Operations**

I think these software options are must-haves because they give emerging businesses total control over the level of customer service and customer experience they provide. Look for CRM and CRX programs designed for the kind of business you have and the capacity you aim for. Invoicing software, such as Zoho Invoice, Invoice by

Wave, Invoice2Go, and Invoice Maker, lets you use your cell phone or a hand-held barcode scanner. There are several others on the market. Compare and select based on your needs. Also, get apps for payment transactions, such as the Square Cash App or Apple Pay. These save time and boost sales by using your cell phone to take credit or debit card payments on the spot.

2. **Social Media**

Social media has transformed marketing and the customer experience in ways never dreamed of, even 20 years ago. It saves businesses both time and money. With Facebook, Instagram, and Twitter, businesses can peek into what their customers think and feel. This means that marketing can be fine-tuned to the customers' actual preferences and pain points. The customer experience can be reshaped to meet the current expectations of the target market and then be further ramped up to "wow" them. Pinterest capitalizes on the tendency of customers to share pictures of what they have purchased—providing free advertising with their collections and boards. LinkedIn has become an excellent platform for businesses to showcase their services and interact with related businesses. Businesses can have their own Facebook and LinkedIn company pages to highlight their specialties and connect with customers. They can even run Facebook and other Ads to bring in more sales.

3. **Online Surveys**

Besides having a customer review section on your e-commerce site or company website, you can find out what your customers and target market think by sending surveys. These surveys can be product- or service-linked, or more general. Never underestimate the value of capturing customer sentiments. Surveys provide helpful feedback so you can improve your products and services based on actual data rather than guessing what your customers like or dislike and hoping you are right. The best way to entice customers to take surveys about their shopping experience is to offer a 10% discount or a free item on their next purchase if they complete the survey. To further convince them to take the time to complete it, let them express their feelings about the product, etc., in a fun way by selecting a smiley face to show how they feel about it:

One effective survey program is Survey Monkey. With it, you can create surveys, polls, or quizzes to measure your customers' responses to your product, service, or any part of your customer experience. Survey Monkey provides convenient templates, so you just fill in your questions. It lets you edit, send and connect seamlessly with your computer, tablet, and phone. You can apply filters to analyze your results better and critique how your products and services satisfy your customers. Each survey has its own link that you can share or send by email to customers.

I love finding out what other successful business minds are thinking. According to Lando Loic, whose expertise is evaluating new tech gadgets and software, "...the right tech tools can help you speed up processes, and as a result, boost productivity." **He recommends some business acceleration tools you might not be aware of, be sure to visit JackiePTaylor.com for the most up-to-date insights.** Technology and providers change rapidly. Some of these organizations may have changed before our publication date!

1. Automate Repetitive Processes. "...[Automating] repetitive and time-consuming tasks like paying your bills or responding to emails is one of the most effective ways technologies can boost productivity in your business and reduce the chance for human errors." How much busy work do you and your employees do every day?

2. Strengthen Marketing

"Today, you can leverage tech tools to create personalized marketing campaigns to target people who need your products/services, thus increasing your chances of converting them into customers and making profits." MobileMonkey keeps you connected to your customers on Instagram, Facebook Messenger, and Web Chat. Besides using Google Analytics to process data, let Ubersuggest speed up your keyword research when you check out the competition!

3. Connect Distributed Teams. Especially since the pandemic, many workforce teams have had to work remotely. Plus, more and more businesses have global operations, and their key employees or clients are in different countries and time zones. There is the technology for that!

Slack is designed to help remote workers stay connected and engaged. It also allows you to integrate apps and bots to streamline the workload. A handy program for scheduling meetings across time zones is Timezone.io.

4. Improve Organization and Collaboration. Working together on critical projects, whether your people are local or spread across the globe, involves sharing information and bouncing ideas off each other. Staying organized, monitoring workflow, and keeping track of all the moving parts can be simplified with Trello or Asana. A great feature of Trello is its Kanban-style boards, which create interactive visuals for team members. Trello can also be integrated with third-party tools to boost productivity: Plus for Trello enables detailed reports; Timeneye does time tracking, and Pomello coordinates with the Pomodoro technique, a time management method.

5. Outsource Tasks to Skilled Professionals. Outsourcing has popped up several times in this book as a cost-effective option for finding qualified freelancers – for a good reason. It is a viable resource for growing your business. Outsourcing allows you to get specific tasks done that your current staff is either too busy to do or require skills outside their fields of expertise.

Loic adds, "You can use platforms like Fiverr to hire skilled freelancers in various categories, including graphic design, writing & translation, video animation, programming & tech, etc." Small individual tasks (gigs) start at $5 and go up.

I would add Upwork.com to the options for outsourcing. It has freelancers with business experience and professional training for larger and more complex jobs.

- As an entrepreneur, finding reasonably priced ways to get specific tasks done will help you immensely as you set up multiple businesses.

> *As an entrepreneur, finding reasonably priced ways to get specific tasks done will help you immensely as you set up multiple businesses.*

Developing Proprietary Technology

We discussed the available enabling technologies to help streamline your operations and improve efficiencies. In addition, technology is available to accelerate your core business. Consider the crux of what you provide, whether you provide a service or product. There is likely technology that can help you do it better, faster, and at a higher volume at a fraction of the cost.

As an emerging business founder, you face a unique set of challenges that make it difficult to compete with established companies. However, developing proprietary technology can potentially help you achieve your goals and create a competitive advantage that can help you thrive.

Proprietary technology refers to a type of technology that is developed and owned by a company and is not available to the general public or competitors.

Proprietary technology can help your businesses differentiate from your competitors. Developing unique and innovative products or services can attract customers looking for something different. Proprietary technology can give your growing business the tools you need to create new and exciting products or services unavailable elsewhere. For example, a small company that develops a new software application that addresses a specific need in the market can gain a competitive advantage over its competitors.

Proprietary technology can help your businesses differentiate from your competitors.

There are several approaches that emerging businesses can take to develop proprietary technology. One method is to hire a team of developers internal to your organization to work on developing new products or services. This approach is typically more expensive but can provide a high degree of control over the development process. Another method is to partner with companies or individuals with the necessary expertise to develop the technology. This approach can be more cost-effective but may require you to give up some control over the development process.

Developing proprietary technology can help your business achieve its goals and create a competitive advantage to help you thrive in an increasingly competitive market. Emerging businesses can gain a foothold in the market and grow their business by differentiating themselves from their competitors, improving their efficiency and productivity, and protecting their intellectual property. There are several approaches to proprietary technology development. Emerging businesses should carefully consider their options to determine which method is best.

Another option is white labeling

White labeling refers to the process of taking a product or service created by one company and rebranding it as your own (removing any references to the original company). Emerging businesses can take advantage of white labeling by partnering with a larger company offering products or services that complement their business offerings. Emerging businesses can expand their product offerings by white labeling their partner's products without investing in product development or manufacturing.

For example, a small marketing agency may white-label a social media management tool from a larger software company and offer it as a service to its clients. The emerging business can rebrand the tool with its logo and branding, making it appear like a tool they have developed themselves. This allows emerging businesses to expand their services and increase revenue without investing in creating their own social media management tool.

White labeling can be a cost-effective way for emerging businesses to offer new products and services to their clients while maintaining control over their branding and customer experience. It can also help them establish themselves as a one-stop shop for their clients' needs, leading to increased customer loyalty and retention.

As your business stretches and grows, technology is the key to keeping your business functioning at the same efficiency level as it did when it was smaller. It may work even more efficiently! By using technology to speed up repetitive tasks and marketing, keep your teams connected and organized, and outsource projects that require skills and time that your workforce doesn't have, you will avoid many of the growing pains that happen when businesses try to expand the old-fashioned way.

Technology can benefit your growing company in several other ways as well. For example, if you know you will rely on additional vendors as your company grows, ensure that your current logistics program can handle the additional shipments. If it can't, explore programs that automate certain aspects of the process. Brainstorm ways technology can make your company's critical systems accomplish their tasks faster and more efficiently.

NOTES

NOTES

-CHAPTER 6-

BOOST! PARTNERSHIPS & COLLABORATIONS

Creating your Alliance Strategy

FOR CENTURIES, THE TRIED-AND-TRUE METHOD of successful business involved a blend of hard work, honesty, a good product or service, clever advertising, and impeccable customer service. Business owners knew that success depended on their efforts and commitment. But in the 21st century, businesses that follow this lone ranger approach have been severely disadvantaged.

The African proverb still rings true today: 'If you want to go fast, go alone; if you want to go far, go together.' By working together, people can accomplish more and achieve greater success than if they work alone. It emphasizes the importance of unity and collaboration in achieving long-term goals. It teaches the value of teamwork and the strength of a collective effort. Today's successful businesses look for partners to help them move to the next level. And it works!

These businesses are creating what we call **strategic partnerships** that enable them to leverage their target market. Also called **strategic alliances,** these voluntary connections have proven to be the solution to every business's growth dilemma sooner or later—how to leverage what they are doing so that the business grows.

Will Kenton, a former senior editor of Investopedia and investment law expert, explains why businesses would even consider alliances with other companies: "A company may enter into a strategic alliance to expand into a new market, improve its product line, or develop an edge over a competitor. The arrangement allows two businesses to work toward a common goal that will benefit both."

And that is the key. **Strategic alliances or partnerships must be a 'win-win' for both parties.** For strategic alliances or partnerships to be successful, both parties must mutually benefit. An example is the partnership between Starbucks and Barnes & Noble, combining their popularity and resources to create a shared location. Barnes & Noble sells books, while Starbucks offers coffee and pastries, all under one roof. This arrangement attracts customers from both companies. Book buyers may also buy coffee, and coffee lovers may leave with a book. Both companies continue to operate independently but pool resources to share location costs and acquire additional customers from both target markets.

So, what exactly is a Strategic Alliance? It is a loose partnership that allows both businesses to maintain their autonomy while joining forces in the areas where it will benefit them both, tangibly and measurably.

SCORE (a resource partner of the SBA-Small Business Administration) encourages businesses to look for ways to partner with other local companies: "A strategic partnership can help your emerging business develop a new product or service, gain exposure to a new target market, raise its brand profile, expand geographically and much more...[Strategic partnerships] can range from relatively minor arrangements, such as co-marketing your products, to more important functions, such as licensing another company's technology to use in the websites you build."

Starbucks also formed a similar strategic alliance with Target as far back as 1999. They based that alliance on their shared customer demographics, adding thousands of Starbucks cafes to Target stores. Today, the thousands of Targets with Starbucks cafes satisfy those customers while significantly boosting sales for both brands.

Strategic alliances are spawned out of creative thinking. Wanting to capitalize on the popularity of the 2019 Super Bowl, Taco Bell, and T-Mobile came up with a promotion that benefited them both. It required forming a strategic alliance: Taco Bell offered a free taco to any T-Mobile customer during the Super Bowl. This encouraged T-Mobile customers to stay with their current plan despite heavy advertising from other providers to switch companies. It worked better than expected. T-Mobile customers rushed to Taco Bell to get their free taco, and most ordered other items, boosting sales for Taco Bell and creating loyal customers.

Strategic partnerships provide added value to customers. Strategic partnerships also enhance the customer experience, as demonstrated by Spotify and Uber teaming up to offer a premium upgrade that allows riders to enjoy personalized playlists during their journeys.

Strategic partnerships can take off if the two businesses share a common incentive. Red Bull and GoPro both have 'adrenaline-seeking' audiences. They partnered in 2012. Red Bull sponsored a breathtaking skydive from a hot air balloon. The skydiver wore a GoPro to record the dive so that viewers could experience the dive with the skydiver. It was such a success on every level that the two companies formed a long-term strategic alliance for all Red Bull extreme sports events. Naturally, only GoPro cameras are used to let viewers experience the events from the athlete's perspective.

Strategic alliances enable businesses to use the newest technology to satisfy their customers. Apple Pay and MasterCard teamed to give more customers additional convenience when making a payment. The Apple Pay system offered contactless transactions—in other words, customers could pay using their iPhone and Mastercard account without needing a physical credit card. Much faster transactions and less hassle for customers. A win-win for customers and both companies.

Imagine if you could partner with another business and, in the process, boost both of your companies forward! But where to start?

SCORE has already written a guideline for establishing your strategic alliance. *It lays out what you need to do to prepare for engaging in a strategic partnership and how to go about setting it up:*

1. **Get your house in order.** *Before you even think about forming a strategic partnership, your business finances, employees, systems, and processes must run smoothly. A strategic partnership isn't a remedy for problems in your business; on the contrary, it will bring them to light.*

2. **Determine your goals.** *What do you want from a strategic partnership? Do you currently sell products regionally and want to partner with a company that has a national sales team to expand your reach? Do you want to offer your customers greater convenience, such as restaurants that partner with Uber to deliver their meals? Do you want access to new manufacturing methods, technologies, or expertise? Knowing what you want from the relationship will help you decide which potential partners to approach.*
3. **Identify potential strategic partners.** *Look for businesses that offer what you need to achieve your goals – they must also share your business's core values. This makes for smoother sailing in the partnership and makes more sense from a branding standpoint. If your business is devoted to social responsibility, for example, you'll want to form strategic partnerships with other companies that share this core value.*
4. **Do your due diligence.** *Before approaching a potential strategic partner, check the company's reputation online, on social media, and among other businesspeople. How strong is their brand? It's also a good idea to contact businesses the company has partnered with and ask about their experiences working together.*
5. **Get to know each other.** *Once you've identified potential strategic partners, use social media and real-life connections to get introduced to key decision-makers. Before you pitch any type of partnership, take time to build*

a relationship. Learn as much as possible about the business's current situation, plans, and long-term goals. This will enable you to identify opportunities and verify that the company is a good fit as a strategic partner.

6. **Make it a win-win.** *Now it's time to propose a strategic partnership. Create a proposal that emphasizes how this relationship will benefit the other company. Of course, it will also benefit you, but that's not what they care about the most.*
7. **Negotiate terms.** *You'll undoubtedly go back and forth as you work out the details of your strategic partnership agreement. No matter how well you know your strategic partner, always create a written agreement to avoid misunderstanding. (This also protects you if your contact at the partner company should leave.) Your contract should detail the nuts and bolts of how the partnership will work. This might include which assets and resources each company will provide, how each firm will be compensated, who is responsible for what, and how the partnership's success will be measured going forward.*
8. **Keep the lines of communication open.** *A strategic partnership isn't something you can 'set and forget,' so don't just sign a paper and go back to business as usual. Both sides must put time and energy into the partnership to get what they want from it. Communicate consistently, hold regular meetings to review the results of your partnership, and make any necessary adjustments.*

You will notice that the businesses that entered the above strategic partnerships were very aware of their **ecosystem**—in other words, they were aware of which businesses were playing in their marketing space. I am not talking about competitors; I am referring to businesses that share a similar target market, supply materials, offer a service you need, or attract customers who also need your products.

For example, businesses occupying a beautician's ecosystem could be: 1. Vendors that provide beauty supplies, 2. Production companies that frequently need makeup and hair done, and 3. Event and wedding planners.

Vendors, production companies, and event planners are examples of **Channel Partners.** Channel partners can funnel multiple resources and customers into your business. Thus, setting up strategic partnerships with them is a wise entrepreneurial move.

Sketch out a schematic of your business's ecosystem and possible channel partners. Then start thinking creatively about innovative partnerships you can form that will help your business grow in ways you hadn't considered before.

Remember that the benefits you receive from a strategic alliance must always be reciprocal. The business you partner with should know they will get what they need from the alliance while they help you achieve your goals. If you think about what you can *give* your potential ally rather than only what you can *receive*, you will have the right priorities to design an amazingly successful strategic alliance that will last a long time and take both of your businesses further than you imagined.

MTM, Inc.

Peg and Lynn Griswold discovered a desperate community need and created a business to meet it. The problem? Patients struggled to find safe and dependable non-emergency medical transportation (NEMT) to medical providers for their appointments, tests, and treatments. The bureaucratic nightmare of Medicare and Medicaid was blocking them from receiving timely services. So, the Griswolds decided that the mission for their company, MTM, Inc., *was to overcome community obstacles and provide these services through a centralized, hassle-free business.*

One of the first things they realized was that they needed to build multiple strategic alliances to achieve these goals. The various organizations and companies whose services they required were not connected—and certainly not in sync with each other. Timing is paramount when trying to transport patients to appointments. All these moving pieces had to be isolated and scheduled so patients wouldn't be left waiting hours without a ride. To accomplish this Herculean feat, the Griswolds worked tirelessly to negotiate and integrate networks of providers.

Over the years, they established a culture of like-minded people committed to removing community barriers for elderly and disadvantaged patients. Located in Lake Saint Louis, MO, *today, 25 years later, under the ownership of* CEO Alaina Maciá, *daughter of the original owners,* MTM, Inc. *can now meet the needs of people anywhere in the* U.S. A Certified Women's Business Enterprise, MTM *now schedules more than* 13 *million non-*

emergency trips each year and has an estimated annual revenue of $675 million as of 2020.

These strategic alliances solidified MTM's hold on market share and enabled the company to grow steadily. In 2021, MTM contracted with a new strategic partner, SAFR, a rideshare service. SAFR is designed to support "women safety and empowerment and is redefining the ridesharing experience." This unique strategic alliance enables MTM to grow exponentially by directly alleviating public fears and ensuring travel safety.

NOTES

-CHAPTER 7-

BOOST! YOUR ACCESS TO CAPITAL

Unique Challenges Faced by Minority, Women, and Veteran Business Owners

IT'S TIME TO FACE REALITY. Not all emerging business owners are up against the same startup or growth challenges. Yes, certain factors exist for all emerging businesses. But if you belong to specific groups or ethnicities, or are a woman or a veteran entrepreneur, you face additional barriers that could interfere with your success and, by extension, your ability to grow your business.

As mentioned in the Introduction, most minority businesses are not family-owned businesses passed down from parents. This means that many minority business owners have never had the chance to experience first-hand how to run a business. They also do not have the benefit of a ready-made customer list. Thus, these startups must start from scratch and figure things out independently.

Historically under-resourced businesses face numerous challenges, perhaps the most critical being access to capital. This issue often prevents these businesses from reaching their full potential and contributes to economic inequalities. In this chapter, we will explore the various obstacles that historically disadvantaged businesses face when seeking capital and several potential solutions.

Many of us are familiar with Oprah Winfrey. She was a T.V. talk show icon in the late 1980s, hosting The Oprah Winfrey Show. Here she bravely tackled topics vital to minorities at that time and got audiences excited about sharing their opinions. But not many people recall or even know that she had a poor start in life. She had a horribly unstable home life where her divorced parents sent her back and forth between them whenever they felt she was out of control or too much of a bother. Worse yet, while she was at her mother's, she was repeatedly molested by male relatives. At the age of 14, Winfrey gave birth to a baby who was premature and did not survive. Finally, she could stay with her father as a teenager and, under his care, became an eager student. Oprah closed the door on her traumatic past and searched for what she was good at. Surprisingly, she discovered that she loved public speaking. Entering a speaking contest, Oprah won a scholarship to Tennessee State University.

During the 1970s, she had opportunities to use that newfound talent when she was hired to work at Nashville's WLAC-TV and Baltimore's WJZ-TV and then to co-host WJZ's People are Talking local talk show. Her talents were showcased when she joined AM Chicago on WLS-TV, a low-rated talk show. Nobody had any expectations that Winfrey could do much with it. Being black and a woman then came with low expectations. Still, Oprah had high expectations of herself; that chance was all she needed. She stunned everyone by turning the show into a resounding success. It was renamed the Oprah Winfrey Show, and Oprah Winfrey became a household name.

But Winfrey wanted to accomplish more. She wasn't satisfied with covering topics the producers told her to. She wanted to make a difference in this world. Oprah started her own production company in 1986, Harpo Productions, so that she could produce shows that covered issues she felt would improve people's lives; her show addressed topics like battered women, alcoholism, and family relationships—subject matter that was previously considered too sensitive to be discussed on T.V. That same year, The Oprah Winfrey Show won three Emmy Awards. Soon her production company had 70 employees and, by 2002, had sales of $314.5 million. In 1988, Harpo Productions became the owner and sole producer of the show. Thus, Oprah became the first woman to own and produce her talk show. Her business ventures took off; by 2003, she had become the first black female billionaire.

While doing all this, Oprah expanded into the publishing industry, setting up her own Book Club in 1996 and launching O Magazine in 2000. These opened up incredible opportunities for her to expand her outreach to minorities and women. The Oprah Winfrey Show continued through 2011. O Magazine moved online in 2020. In 2021, Oprah further proved she was a true entrepreneur by launching her own cable T.V. network, OWN (Oprah Winfrey Network). It is jointly owned by Warner Bros. Discovery and Harpo Studios and replaced the Discovery Health Channel. This fulfilled her dream of providing messaging and entertainment explicitly targeting the African-American viewership's needs and interests.

Throughout all the zigzags of her career, Oprah Winfrey proved that she could stay true to her values and be a successful entrepreneur with her productions and philanthropy. She has personally donated millions of dollars to charities, especially The Angel Network, The Oprah Winfrey Foundation, and The Oprah Winfrey Operating Foundation. Oprah received the Presidential Medal of Freedom in 2013 for philanthropy.

Oprah is an amazing example of overcoming the odds and succeeding against obstacles.

For centuries, individuals from marginalized communities have experienced significant barriers that have hindered their ability to access financial services. These barriers include discriminatory lending practices, lack of collateral, and limited financial planning skills. The impacts of these inequalities have been profound. Historically under-resourced businesses often face a more comprehensive range of financial pressures than other businesses, including dealing with higher-than-average interest rates, difficulty securing loans, and limited investment opportunities.

Despite these challenges, several potential solutions exist for businesses to obtain the necessary capital to grow and expand.

One such solution is **crowdfunding**, a process that involves soliciting contributions from many investors via digital platforms, often social media. Crowdfunding provides access to capital without relying on traditional lending institutions, allowing businesses to secure funding without meeting stringent requirements.

Another solution is seeking **business grants**, which provide some businesses with financial assistance to grow. This type of funding does not need to be repaid. It is designed to assist companies that may not qualify for loans, allowing those from under-resourced backgrounds to level the playing field.

Additionally, **loans** provide access to capital without requiring equity stakes or forfeiting company control. This can be done through traditional SBA or other lending institutions. Loans are particularly beneficial to those who are just starting a business or looking to expand and provide an opportunity for businesses to access capital without having to give up ownership or ultimate decision-making power.

Finally, **equity investments, or venture capital,** are investments made in a company in exchange for an ownership stake or a percentage of future earnings. Typically used by more established businesses, equity investments are high-risk and high-reward, providing capital in exchange for a significant return on investment. However, for historically under-resourced companies, it can be challenging to find the right investor as they often have specific criteria for allocating their funds.

The combination of discriminatory financial practices, lack of collateral, and financial planning skills has resulted in significant financial constraints, making it more challenging to access financial services. However, solutions such as crowdfunding, grants, and loans may offer easier access to capital, allowing businesses that come from under-resourced backgrounds to invest in their progress and expansion. By reducing financial inequalities, historically disadvantaged companies have a more level playing field, and society benefits from many thriving businesses.

The good news is that business accelerators are available for emerging businesses like yours. The bad news is that minorities are usually **over-mentored** and **under-monetized.** Over-mentored means that many organizations offer advice and guidelines for building a successful business. Unfortunately, much of that advice does not fit the realities that these business owners face daily. Under-monetized means that funding opportunities are frequently out of reach for these groups.

A **business accelerator** is a specialized program intended to assist small startups or businesses in their beginning stages, which have the potential to expand at a rapid rate. The program is typically time-based, usually for a few months to years, and helps entrepreneurs acquire resources, knowledge, guidance, and financing essential for success. Accelerators provide office spaces, training, networking, and funding opportunities, and the selection process is highly competitive.

I'm often asked, "Business accelerators sound great but who is offering these programs?" To understand the universe of programs that exist in this space, I've outlined them below.

1. Large corporations establish **corporate accelerators** to aid start-ups that align with their business goals.
2. **Government accelerators** are established by governmental organizations to support start-ups in crucial sectors for the nation's economic growth.

3. **Industry-specific accelerators** are designed to provide particular guidance and support to start-ups in designated markets, such as healthcare or financial services.
4. **Incubators** offer early-stage start-ups resources, networking opportunities, and office space.
5. **Venture capital accelerators** funded by venture capital organizations offer mentorship and funding in exchange for equity to start-ups.
6. **Community accelerators**, which cater to all start-ups in a particular area, offer resources and assistance to help them thrive.
7. **Hybrid accelerators** combine elements from various acceleration types, such as merging industry-specific emphasis with venture capital funding.

Taking advantage of available programs:

It's a good idea to get as much knowledge as possible before starting your business or trying to grow it. To support this, many business incubators and startup programs are available online and through local chambers of commerce that fall into the category of business acceleratorMany of my mentees will ask how they should select which program(s) are the best use of their time.

Generally, these accelerators fall into four types of programs are available to entrepreneurs through public sector sources or private sector organizations: **Business Mentoring, Capacity-Building, Monetary, and Hybrid (a mix of the three)**. Before you sign up for any of them, consider what areas you need help with and evaluate them in light of your specific needs.

Business Mentoring programs will guide you through starting or growing your_business. One well-rounded public mentoring program is "SCORE." SCORE, being a partner of the Small Business Administration (SBA), offers mentoring possibilities and grants access to essential programs and financing tailored for minority groups through its website. The SBA is dedicated to helping your business thrive for years. Its local mentoring chapters provide emerging businesses with much-needed connections and support.

There are also mentoring programs that help you develop as an entrepreneur: "According to SCORE, 87% of entrepreneurs with a mentor are still in business after one year, compared to 75% of those without a mentor." Don't be afraid to ask for advice from people who are where you want to be.

The private sector also offers a host of mentorship and hybrid programs to help businesses in the startup and more mature stages of their growth journey.

Mentorship and capacity-building programs for emerging businesses are two types of support programs that offer different services to emerging business owners. Mentorship programs are designed to provide guidance, support, and expertise to emerging business owners through a structured relationship between a mentor and a mentee. Capacity-building programs are focused on helping emerging businesses generate revenue and profitability through various strategies and tactics.

In mentorship programs, a business owner can access the experience, knowledge, and expertise of a mentor who has been in the industry for an extended period. Mentors help business owners develop their skills, competencies, and networks. Mentors also provide feedback and support to the business owner, which can be invaluable in growing and building a successful business and connecting founders to key relationships.

On the other hand, monetary programs focus on directly providing revenue upon program completion or generating revenue and profitability through marketing, advertising, and other business techniques. These programs help emerging businesses grow their customer base, increase sales, and improve overall profitability. Monetary programs might include strategies such as selling products, offering services, developing a membership program or subscription service, and creating digital products or e-books.

In summary, mentorship programs focus on personal and professional development, while monetary programs focus on generating revenue and profitability. Both programs can be valuable for emerging businesses, depending on their needs and goals.

A Capacity-building program is different from mentoring

Capacity-building programs for emerging businesses are specialized training and support programs designed to help emerging businesses improve their operations and increase their overall effectiveness.

Some examples of capacity-building programs for emerging businesses include:

1. **Business Management Training**: These programs provide entrepreneurs with the skills to manage their businesses better and successfully operate.

2. **Financial Management Training**: These programs offer training in developing financial management strategies, including managing cash flow, financial analysis, and tax planning.
3. **Marketing and Sales Training:** These programs teach emerging business owners to develop and implement effective marketing and sales strategies to promote their products and services.
4. **Technology Support and Training**: These programs offer assistance to emerging businesses to upgrade their technology infrastructure and learn how to use new software and tools effectively.
5. **Leadership and Team Building Training**: These programs focus on developing leadership skills to help emerging business owners and their employees become more effective.
6. **Understanding Access to Capital**: These programs provide emerging businesses with funding opportunities that can enable them to grow their operations.
7. **Networking and Partnership Opportunities**: These programs allow emerging business owners to network with other entrepreneurs, business leaders, and experts in different fields to learn new skills and access more resources.

Minorities in Business, a support group in Missouri, aims to supply those needs. They define capacity-building as "offering...technical assistance and a variety of business and wealth building educational opportunities in collaboration with our local and regional business resource partners." Their goal is "to increase the number of minority-owned businesses in the Springfield Missouri area that can successfully compete for government-funded procurement/contracts as a certified MBE [Minority Business Enterprise], WBE [Woman Business Enterprise], and/or DBE [Disadvantaged Business Enterprise]."[3]

Search for capacity-building programs that have local networking groups near you. They have already studied the economic challenges in your area and can connect you with educational resources, grant and loan opportunities, and local business owners who can encourage you with their own experience and success. They comprise other local business owners who have already gone through what you are going through. The Small Business Administration (SCORE) can also put you in touch with a local networking group. It can provide additional support for you with online courses and links to grants and loans.

An often-unnoticed aspect of capacity-building is what to do if suddenly your business takes off and you are flush with cash. We have all heard about people who suddenly became millionaires by winning the lottery but who blew through their money and were broke again in a year or so. You are probably telling yourself, "Well, that wouldn't be me," but are you sure? In addition to having an experienced financial advisor and legal advisor, seeking out and interacting with entrepreneurs who have experienced this can help you be ready to handle exponentially growing your business.

There will be a time when each of these mentoring programs will be of value to you. You have to determine when you need which ones you need and when.

Veterans:

Veterans also struggle in this area of capital. Many have no support system when they are discharged from the military. So, it is unsurprising that they struggle to get their business off the ground.

"The largest barrier to entrepreneurship among Veterans is access to capital. In 2019, 41% of 'vetrepreneurs' could not secure any funding for their business." "Although the number of female 'vetrepreneurs' is growing, the vast majority are male (93%) and white (81%)."

Yet, despite these barriers, "Veteran business owners accounted for 6.1% (351,237) of all U.S. employer businesses, and employ approximately 4 million workers."—a fantastic accomplishment.

Native Americans:

An often-forgotten minority is the Native Americans. These business owners and entrepreneurs face financial and legal challenges in setting up and succeeding with their businesses. The Office of Native American Affairs, a department of the SBA, is dedicated to meeting those needs. They provide multiple financing options and educational resources on their website. Check it out at https://www.sba.gov/business-guide/grow-your-business/native-american-owned-businesses

Also,"[the] Department of the Interior's Bureau of Indian Affairs provides services to federally recognized tribes.... [Education], job training, and employment opportunities...are delivered through contracts, grants, and compacts to approximately 1.9 million American Indians and Alaska Natives."

Accelerating Access to Business Funding

There is a little-known action that you, as a minority business owner, can do to access multiple governmental and private sector funding resources and other benefits. If you **receive certification as a minority-owned business**, you will gain access to minority business grants, be able to apply for government contracts, and qualify as a supplier for larger companies. Certifications are available from a variety of sources, visit www.JackiePTaylor.com for details.

Four distinct designations help to qualify a small business for financial aid and business opportunities: MBE [Minority Business Enterprise], 8(a) Business Development designation, WBE [Woman Business Enterprise], and DBE [Disadvantaged Business Enterprise]." If qualified, it is worth taking time to get one of these designations because it opens you up to grant and loan opportunities and puts you on a list of potential suppliers for governmental and large corporation contracts, which can help you build capacity and take your business to the next level. Note, the term "small" business is used in this section as it is a descriptor with criteria attached to it. You have to meet "small business" criteria to be eligible for some of these designations. For example, The Small Business Administration manages the 8(a) Business Development Program, which aims to empower small and underprivileged businesses to compete in the American marketplace and gain access to federal procurement opportunities. The program caters to companies that are at least 51% owned and managed by socially or economically disadvantaged individuals, and it offers a wide range of support services, including specialized business training, counseling, marketing aid, and top-tier executive development. Qualified businesses can also benefit from sole-source government contracts valued up to $4 million for goods and services or up to $6.5 million for manufacturing. The certification duration is initially nine years, with the possibility for extensions.

Here are 10 potential sources who can GIVE A BOOST! to founders looking to grow and scale their businesses. Additional resources are provided at www.JackiePTaylor.com

1. **Y Combinator:** Y Combinator is a startup accelerator that provides seed funding, mentorship, and resources to early-stage startups. Benefits include access to a vast alumni network, investors, mentors, and possibly investment from Y Combinator itself. Eligibility is open to startups at any stage. https://www.ycombinator.com/
2. **Microsoft for Startups**: Microsoft for Startups provides access to tools, resources, and support for startups building on Microsoft technologies. Benefits include access to Azure credits, technical support, and go-to-market resources. Eligibility is open to startups who use Microsoft technologies in their products. https://startups.microsoft.com/
3. **Google Launchpad:** Google Launchpad is a startup accelerator that provides mentorship, resources, and access to Google's network to help startups scale. Benefits include access to Google Cloud credits, mentorship, and technical support. Eligibility is open to startups with a product and initial traction. https://launchpad.google.com/

4. **Techstars:** Techstars is a global startup accelerator that provides seed funding, mentorship, and access to a vast network of mentors, investors, and alumni. Benefits include access to resources, mentorship, and potential investment from Techstars. Eligibility is open to early-stage startups. https://www.techstars.com/
5. **MassChallenge:** MassChallenge is a non-profit startup accelerator that provides mentorship, resources, and access to a vast network of mentors and investors. Benefits include access to resources, mentorship, and a chance to win cash prizes. Eligibility is open to any startup at any stage. https://masschallenge.org/
6. **500 Startups**: 500 Startups is a global venture capital firm and startup accelerator that provides seed funding, mentorship, and resources to early-stage startups. Benefits include access to a vast network of alumni, investors, mentors, and possibly investment from 500 Startups. Eligibility is open to startups at any stage, including pre-seed or post-revenue. https://500.co/
7. **Amplify LA:** Amplify LA is a startup accelerator that provides mentorship, resources, and access to a vast network of investors and mentors. Benefits include access to resources, mentorship, and potential investment. Eligibility is open to early-stage startups in the technology or media industries. https://amplify.la/
8. **Intel Capital Innovators:** Intel Capital Innovators is a startup accelerator that provides mentorship, resources, and a chance to work with Intel. Benefits include access to resources, mentorship,

and potential investment from Intel. Eligibility is open to early-stage startups in the technology industry. https://www.intelcapital.com/startups/innovators

9. **The Brandery**: The Brandery is a startup accelerator focusing on marketing and branding. Benefits include mentorship and access to a vast network of alumni and investors. Eligibility is open to early-stage startups in the technology, consumer packaged goods, or e-commerce industries. https://www.brandery.org/

10. **PayPal Incubator:** PayPal Incubator is a startup accelerator that provides mentorship, resources, and access to a vast network of investors and mentors. Benefits include access to PayPal's user base, mentorship, and resources. Eligibility is open to early-stage fintech. https://www.paypal.com/incubator

Benetrends is an online service that lists resources for minority-owned businesses and links to them. Here are some examples.

- "The U.S. Small Business Administration (SBA) provides funding opportunities for minority-owned businesses and helpful tools to guide your business at each stage of its development.
- The SBA's 8(a) Business Development Program is designed to provide a level playing field to small businesses owned by socially and economically disadvantaged people. The program offers access to set-asides by government agencies.
- The SBA's Emerging Leaders Initiative operates in 60 cities, delivering executive-level

entrepreneurship training. The seven-month program provides access to mentors, specialized workshops, and access to peers, civic leaders, and the financial community.

- The Minority Business Development Agency awards prizes that average $300,000 for renewable project grants.
- The Native American Business Development Institute gives grants to strengthen economic growth among Native American and Alaskan Native business owners in their communities.
- The U.S. Department of Health and Human Services gives grants to businesses that work to improve health issues among historically disenfranchised populations.
- Federal Express sponsors an annual small-business grant contest and awards 10 prizes of $25,000 each."

Maybe your entrepreneurial spirit has been beaten down by obstacles blocking your way. Hopefully, this chapter has given you hope that help is available. You just have to reach out and grab it!

NOTES

-CHAPTER 8-

BOOST! YOUR GRITTINESS

(Characteristics of a "Winning" Entrepreneur!)

ENTREPRENEURSHIP CAN BE A DAUNTING and challenging path. Still, it can be a rewarding and fulfilling journey for those who possess the power of grit and determination. **Grit is a unique blend of passion, resilience, perseverance, and focus that helps individuals overcome obstacles and achieve long-term goals.**

When we talk about grit in entrepreneurship, we refer to successful entrepreneurs' tenacity and determination. These individuals remain steadfast in the face of failure, rejection, and uncertainty and keep pushing forward until they achieve success.

One of the hallmarks of a successful entrepreneur is the ability to maintain a strong and positive mindset in the face of adversity. This means having a growth mindset where failure and setbacks are seen as opportunities for learning and growth. Entrepreneurs with this mindset can quickly bounce back from failures and use the experience to their advantage. They do not view failure as a reflection of their personal worth but as a natural part of the entrepreneurial journey. Instead of giving up when faced with setbacks, they use these experiences to refine their approach, refine their strategy, and look for new opportunities.

Along with a strong mindset, successful entrepreneurs also possess a set of specific habits that enable them to persevere through difficult times. These habits include discipline, determination, and a willingness to take calculated risks. Entrepreneurs who possess these habits are focused and dedicated to their goals, are willing to put in the time and effort required to succeed and are willing to take calculated risks to seize opportunities. They are ready to pivot and make changes when faced with obstacles and are not afraid to try new things.

The power of grit and determination is essential for success in entrepreneurship. It takes more than a good idea or a desire for success to make it in this industry. Entrepreneurs who possess the traits of grit and determination can overcome obstacles, learn from failures, and achieve their long-term goals. By adopting the same mindset and habits as successful entrepreneurs, we can develop the grit and determination we need to overcome our challenges and succeed in our entrepreneurial journeys. Ultimately, success in entrepreneurship is not just about talent or luck but about having the courage to get gritty and persevere through the most challenging times.

Getting "Gritty" means being brutally honest about your attitude, tendencies and abilities. Be honest about your business, too. You can't get to where you want to be if you don't know where you are starting from.

So, start with yourself

List your personal strengths and weaknesses. Remember—be brutally honest. **Everyone has Personal Barriers that keep us from achieving our dreams.** They often take the form of fears. **Four Fears** trip up many novice entrepreneurs:

1. Fear of trying new things,
2. Fear of failure,
3. Fear of criticism, and
4. Fear of not having enough time to do it all.

As you imagine yourself as a successful entrepreneur, do any of these fears make you worry that you might be unable to do this?

Are you the type of person who jumps at opportunities or would you rather wait and think about it for (quite) a while? →*You may have the fear of trying new things.*

Have you had so many false starts that you suspect that this new venture might fail right out of the gate, too? →*You have a fear of failure.*

Do you worry that if you try this new idea, your spouse, colleague or parent might knock it down as impossible? →*You have a fear of criticism.*

Are you so overworked now that you can't imagine adding one more thing to your plate? →*You have a fear of not having enough time.*

The first step in being an entrepreneur is identifying your natural fears and telling yourself that you will do whatever it takes to remove the triggers for those fears. So, approach new opportunities with a cheerful "*I can do this!*" attitude. Remember that Thomas Edison failed at designing a working lightbulb 1000 times before he succeeded—butbecause he was persistent, he transformed the world! If other people shoot down your idea, ignore them because they don't have the same knowledge, passion and inner drive that you do. If you panic at the thought of overloading yourself, remember you are not alone. There are mentors, talented people and fantastic technology that will help you accomplish much more, faster and better than you could in the past.

What qualities do all winning entrepreneurs have? Below are some positive traits that they share. See how many of these traits you have and where you fall short. Think about why that is and how you can change yourself to become what you want.

- ☐ **Strong leadership qualities**
- ☐ **Highly self-motivated**
- ☐ **Strong sense of basic ethics and integrity**
- ☐ **Willingness to fail**
- ☐ **Serial innovators**
- ☐ **Know what you don't know**
- ☐ **Competitive spirit**
- ☐ **Understand the value of a strong peer network**

This fascinating list appeared in a blog from the **Minority Business Development Agency** in Washington, DC. Most of these traits are self-explanatory, but the writer of the blog made a few critical points that I want to share with you:

<u>Trait #1</u>: Are you the kind of leader who can "amass a team of people toward a common goal so that the entire team is motivated and works effectively to get there"?

Trait #4: "Successful entrepreneurs are risk-takers who...are not afraid of failure." A true entrepreneur will ask, "What if [we tried this]?"

Trait #5: "Entrepreneurs are almost defined by their drive to develop new ideas and improve on existing processes constantly." Maybe it's a character flaw, but they have an insatiable desire to build a better mousetrap. And then they find a way to turn that mousetrap into a new product or business!

Trait #6: Entrepreneurs are not "know it all." They are keenly aware of what they know and don't know. So, they are always searching for answers and for people who have those answers.

This prepares them for Trait #8: They understand that "...it takes a network of contacts, business partners, financial partners, peers and resources to succeed." They "nurture these relationships and surround themselves with people who can help make them more effective."

Kelsey Miller, in her blog for Harvard Business School Online, has a few additional traits that you need to be aware of. These come from the Entrepreneurship Essentials course offered by HBS:

1. ***Curiosity.*** *Successful entrepreneurs have a sense of curiosity that allows them to continuously seek new opportunities.*
2. ***Structured Experimentation.*** *You "need to conduct thorough market research and run meaningful tests to validate your idea and determine whether it has potential."*
3. ***Persistence.*** *Entrepreneurs don't give up easily. "...[They] see failures as opportunities to learn and grow."*

4. **Risk Tolerance.** *This fits with the "willingness to fail" that we discussed earlier. If you bake the chance of failing into your plan, you won't be thrown off track if it happens. Instead, you will find a creative way to develop a better option.*
5. **Long-Term Focus.** "[It's] *easy to start a business, but hard to grow a sustainable and substantial one...Entrepreneurship is a long-term endeavor," whether you are growing one business or several.*

So, how do you rate yourself on these entrepreneurial traits? Do they all come naturally to you, or do you think you may have to work on some of them?

____

____

____

____

____

____

Zoom

Today's employees don't think twice about being part of a Zoom call meeting. It's just one of the conveniences of today's technology. But Zoom didn't just materialize out of thin air. The idea for Zoom was sparked by one man's attempt to solve a personal problem and only arose because of his positive entrepreneurial success mindset.

Eric Yuan grew up in China. Although an avid student, he wasn't satisfied with the education he was receiving there. He saw America as his chance to succeed in life. But getting a visa presented a significant problem. It took him two full years and eight tries to finally obtain that visa. Once here, he attended Stanford University Graduate School of Business. After graduation, Eric worked in Silicon Valley. A brilliant engineer, Eric was one of the founders of a communication startup and proved crucial to the success of its online meetings product. He later became VP of Engineering at WebEx, an online meetings platform. When Cisco acquired WebEx in 2007, Eric was promoted to VP of Engineering at the new Cisco Webex.

Although happy with his career, Eric had a personal dilemma. His girlfriend lived 10 hours away by train. Eric wondered if there might be a way for him to see his girlfriend more often without making the long trip. His expertise in communication platforms got him thinking about creating a video conferencing app. That way, he and his girlfriend could see each other anytime through their computers. Even more importantly, this platform could connect businesses and clients worldwide with a few clicks. It was a fantastic idea! So, he presented it to Cisco. To his dismay, they rejected it outright. But Eric knew that it was a great idea. Unfazed by the rejection, he built his own video conferencing platform, founded Zoom and became its CEO.

Eric had a true entrepreneur's success mindset. He combined his experience, talent and determination to succeed in the face of repeated rejection to take Zoom from a dream to a business platform that changed the face of communication. Within the first five months of activation, Zoom *was already used by one million users. In January 2019, Zoom launched its cloud telephone service (Zoom Phone). This pivotal moment transformed this web meeting app into a comprehensive business communication service. Eric didn't stop there. During the pandemic, when many businesses experienced slowdowns, Eric acquired Keybase. This end-to-end encryption (E2EE) tool provided secure messaging and file-sharing, a feature that lured companies. Later that year, Zoom expanded this service so that E2EE could be used for meetings of up to 200 participants. Today, Zoom is valued at around $110 billion.*

TO DO: *Grab your list of personal strengths and weaknesses. Add your thoughts on which of the winning entrepreneurial traits you have and which ones you want.*

It would be so much easier if everyone who wanted to become an entrepreneur already had all the right qualities. However, like any area of expertise, some may be innate - yet the rest must be learned, developed and practiced.

Are you willing to equip yourself to be a successful entrepreneur? If so, then make a personal plan to acquire more of those traits and develop the ones you have.

Always build on your strengths and find ways to build up the areas where you are weaker. As we mentioned in this book, team up with people with those strengths and rely on their expertise as you grow your business and work toward the future.

Teams You Can Depend On:

1. Your "Pit Crew." When NASCAR drivers race around the track, they frequently have to make a pit stop to get a tire changed or another quick repair done so that they can continue the race. These mechanics, the pit crew, are experts at what they do, and the driver depends on them to get the car back on track. The experts on your team are your Pit Crew too. As owner or CEO of your company and leader of your team, you have to depend on your experts to give you the facts you either don't know or don't have time to find out. Moreover, their talents and skills in their particular fields allow you to rely on them 100% as you make decisions based on their input.
2. Your "Mastermind Circle." This is an ever-widening group of experts outside your company that you learn from. This circle includes online and local business mentors who have been through what you are going through and are happy to share their hard-earned wisdom with you. Also in this group are your strategic partners with whom you have joined forces to compete and win over your total share of the market. The blessing in all this is that, over time, you become part of other entrepreneurs' master circles and can help them as well.

As you grow your business and plan for your future, write down the names of these individuals in your "pit crew" and "master circle" and their special skills. Then find ways to show them your appreciation for how they are helping you stay strong, stay on track and reach your entrepreneurial dream.

My "Pit Crew" (internal)		My Mastermind Circle (external)		
Name	Internal Expertise	Name	Company/ Organization	Expertise

NOTES

NOTES

BOOST! IT'S A VERB...SO TAKE ACTION

I BET THAT PARTS OF this book spoke to you. Specific insights may even have jumped out at you as you realized that you found the answer you've been looking for!

I now challenge you to start working on the aspects of growing your business and being an entrepreneur that are important to you.

Your success so far has proven that you have what it takes to accomplish way more than you think you can! All you have to do now is implement the steps to move your business from where you are to where you want it to go. Visit JackiePTaylor.com to access the forms and templates to support the below action steps and obtain the most up-to-date access to worksheets, resources, opportunities and events. Join our Business Boost! Community.

- Define your WHY: Complete the Legacy questions in the Introduction of this book.
- Access a copy of the SWOT analysis at www.JackiePTaylor.com and complete it to see what your business is doing well and where you need to make changes.
- Download a template for a business growth plan and explore the possibilities for your company at JackiePTaylor.com.

- Use the three types of programs available to entrepreneurs: Small Business Mentoring, Capacity-Building and Monetary, to grow your business and equip you to handle the challenges you will face.
- Seek out financing possibilities, especially the ones for minorities, veterans and women, by visiting the RESOURCES page at www.JackiePTaylor.com
- Make your workforce your priority. Equip your workforce with the right training and enabling technologies. Support them by providing adequate resources and autonomy, and by letting them know how critical they are to the future success of your company. Complete the workforce template on www.JackiePTaylor.com
- Read over the areas where technology can BOOST! your business ahead. (Chapter 5)
- Explore forming Strategic Alliances to move your business to the next level.
- Discover how many traits you already have that you share with winning entrepreneurs! Start cultivating more of them.

How have the insights in this book applied to your business growth strategy? What elements of your business need to be changed or enhanced to grow and scale?

List the resources you plan to use to prepare yourself and your business so that you can scale it and become a true entrepreneur. Don't forget to access the resources at www.JackiePTaylor.com

____

____

____

____

____

____

Create a long-term plan for your future as an entrepreneur. Access the planning template at www.JackiePTaylor.com.

In the meantime, get started with the prompts below.

Document any challenges that you face as a historically under-resourced entrepreneur. The goal is not to dwell on the obstacles but to acknowledge them and develop a plan for what you will do to mitigate them. List challenges and mitigation.

____

____

____

____

____

____

What are you passionate about? How do you translate that passion to your employees, partners, etc.? Make it plain. It's essential that they understand and can share in your vision, too.

Action breeds more action. Create a short-term plan for what you will do today, tomorrow, and over the next few weeks to make your dream of being an entrepreneur a reality! We'll get you started.

TODAY:

TOMORROW:

Week 1:

Week 2:

NOTES

ABOUT JACKIE P TAYLOR

Diversity Enthusiast. Guided By Passion. Energized By Helping Others.

JACKIE P. TAYLOR IS A leading global executive, business strategist and dynamic motivational speaker who has inspired audiences for over 20 years. With her unique blend of passion and expertise in the business world, Jackie has become a go-to source for business insights and motivation.

Jackie P. Taylor, also known as the 'Business Boost! Doctor' serves as a senior Partner with a renowned big four global consulting firm and has spent the last 20+ years working with government leaders, global executives, and growing business founders, helping them translate their strategies into operationalization that makes sense. She has served as a coach and thought partner for Fortune 500 executives and senior leaders responsible for billion-dollar budgets. She has mentored numerous business owners, sharing with them strategic business insights on how to grow and scale business operations. Her ability to break down complicated concepts and distill them into simple solutions makes her a sought-after resource in the business community.

Jackie has shared her inspiring insights and experiences at countless events, inspiring c-suite executives, government leaders and entrepreneurs alike. Her focus on growing and scaling businesses, embracing failure, and sharing proven pathways to operationalizing organizational initiatives resonates with her audience, giving business leaders the courage and motivation to challenge themselves, build strong teams, and create meaningful business impact. www.JackiePTaylor.com

Jackie is a devoted mother, godmother and mentor. She is actively involved in various community initiatives, including championing adoption and foster care, promoting diversity, equity, and inclusion, advocating for health equity, and supporting economic development by expanding workforce and emerging businesses. She generously donates her time and skills to make a tangible difference in the lives of others.

www.ingramcontent.com/pod-product-compliance
Lightning Source LLC
Chambersburg PA
CBHW071942190726
48293CB00004B/1310

* 9 7 8 1 9 5 5 1 0 7 8 1 5 *